Letts

A-level
In a Week

Sociology

AQA

Year 2

**Andy Bennett,
Scott Keifer and
Matthew Wilkin**

CONTENTS

In Paper 2 (Topics in Sociology), you will need to answer questions on The Media **or** Beliefs in Society – not both. Ask your teacher for more information about the assessment breakdown.

Beliefs in Society: Perspectives on Religion

Views on religion in the sociological world can be divided into those that see religion as a good/positive institution and those that are critical of its role in society. For example, functionalists see religion as helping to form consensus in society by bringing groups of people together. However, Marxists and feminists believe that religion acts as a conservative force by holding individuals in a system of **hegemony**. Postmodernism looks at religion in a contemporary way by examining the role it plays in societies today.

Functionalist Views – Religion Provides a Collective Conscience

The functionalist Emile Durkheim believed that religion can give people a sense of belonging and a shared identity; he referred to this as a **collective conscience.** Durkheim studied tribes in central Australia and the practice of **totemism**, and he identified that objects can become symbolic and bring people together. Other functionalists such as Malinowski and Parsons agree that religion is a key institution in the socialisation process by providing people with a sense of direction and a moral order which keeps individuals from engaging in criminal or deviant behaviour. Parsons states that religion can help during times of instability or crisis and therefore acts as an essential provider of values. The New Right supports many of the functionalist views by identifying how religion can act as a mechanism for stability and maintaining traditional values.

EVALUATION POINT

Although functionalist ideas on religion are still important, they are often seen as outdated. Religion played a greater role in society when Durkheim was writing (1912). Many would argue that the media has replaced religion as a key component of socialisation.

Marxist Views – Religion and the Function of Hegemony

Marx famously said that religion is the "opium of the people", by which he meant that religion was used like a drug to justify the hierarchy of a society and maintain the unfair social imbalance between the rich and poor. Other Marxists such as Althusser believe that religion is part of the **ideological state apparatus**, consisting of the institutions that maintain social inequality and the dominant positions of class and power by justifying the suffering of the poor as inevitable. Likewise, Gramsci developed the idea of **hegemony** by stating that religion maintains upper-class dominance by justifying the place that working-class individuals find themselves in. Marxists believe that religion acts to maintain both hegemony and capitalism from one generation to the next.

EVALUATION POINT

Marxism provides an insight into why the proletariat often use religion to help them in life. However, Marxism fails to explain why religion is often a key part of the lives of many of those from the middle and upper classes. Religion is sometimes a choice and not forced upon the individual.

The Protestant Ethic and the Spirit of Capitalism

The ideas of Max Weber (1904) supported many Marxist theories by relating social-class inequality to religion. Weber studied a group of protestants called Calvinists, and noted that they believed that a hard work ethic could help them to get a place in heaven by being one of the chosen few. Therefore, Weberian theory states that the roots of capitalism can be traced to the values of hard work, modesty and business ideas associated with early Protestantism.

Weber stated that religion acted as a catalyst for capitalism, which resulted in social change. However, Marxists and functionalists argue that religion actually maintains the norm rather than acting as a force for change. For functionalists this reinforces a collective conscience, but for Marxists it reinforces class conflict in society.

Patriarchy in Religion

Feminist sociologists believe that religion acts as a tool to maintain **patriarchy** and the dominance of males. Theorists such as De Beauvoir and El-Saadawi believe that Christianity and Islam both promote the traditional roles of females as wives and mothers; females are portrayed as either virginal and pure or as sinners. Feminists also argue that females are marginalised by religion as the scriptures often portray them as less important or less powerful than their male counterparts. Indeed, in many religious organisations females are in positions of less responsibility or are expected to perform stereotypical roles.

It is important to understand that there are different strands of feminist views of religion; for example, liberal feminists differ in their views compared to radical, Black and Marxist feminists. Changes within religions which embrace equality (for instance, the introduction of female priests) show progress, which is noted by liberal feminists.

Postmodernism and Religion

The postmodern view starts by recognising that many perspectives are now outdated and that in contemporary globalised societies religion now plays a less important role. Sociologists such as Bauman noted that many humans have lost faith in religious explanations of the world and that there is an increase in individualism, diversity and freedom of choice from the religious and spiritual ideas on offer; Bauman calls this **liquid modernity**. Other postmodernists such as Bruce discuss the postmodern world in terms of **secularisation**, in that as countries progress and develop they are less likely to rely on religion; developments in science also add to the fragmentation of major religious beliefs.

The postmodern view highlights the growth of secularisation in many parts of the world. However, it must also be noted that fundamentalism is on the rise in other parts of the world.

SUMMARY

- Sociological perspectives on religion fall into those that see religion as positive and those that see religion as negative.

- Functionalists see religion as providing consensus, while Marxists and feminists see religion as a form of conflict, and they also recognise its ability to prevent social change.

- Functionalists and New Right sociologists believe that religion is good for society as it provides consensus and a collective conscience.

- Marxists believe that religion legitimises and maintains social inequality.

- Weberian theory believes that religion can act as a mechanism for social change and was the catalyst for capitalism.

- Feminists believe that religion perpetuates and maintains the system of patriarchy.

- Different groups of feminism focus on different examples of patriarchy within religions.

- Postmodernists believe that globalisation has caused religion to be more individualised and has also accelerated secularisation.

QUICK TEST

1. What is meant by consensus and conflict approaches to religion?

2. What is meant by totemism?

3. Which Marxist discussed the ideas of the ideological state apparatus?

4. What word describes the idea of maintaining leadership and dominance by those in power?

5. Calvinism belongs to which religious belief system?

6. What is meant by religion being a conservative force?

7. What is meant by the marginalisation of women in religion?

8. Which postmodernist discussed ideas on liquid modernity?

9. Define what is meant by secularisation?

10. What does Durkheim suggest can happen when religious objects take on a meaning which is shared by members of society?

PRACTICE QUESTIONS

Question 1: Outline and explain two ways in which feminists believe that religion maintains the system of patriarchy. (10 marks) **Spend 15 minutes on your response.**

HINTS TO HELP YOU RESPOND

You need to make sure that your response has two very different examples and each one is of equal length. Remember that there are different types of feminism and so focusing on two different disciplines of feminism would be beneficial as this will ensure your two points are not too similar to each other. In aiming to add two different points you may use liberal feminist views citing the example of female priests and noting that this allows some women to escape patriarchal control and gain freedom and respect. You could also note the radical feminist views of De Beauvoir and El-Saadawi in stating that religion simply reinforces patriarchal stereotypes of the role of women in society.

Item A

Many sociologists believe that religion – along with the family and education – is one of the key institutions in society to provide consensus and a sense of solidarity. However, other commentators argue that religion has caused more harm than good and that it actually acts as a form of conflict rather than consensus.

Question 2: Applying material from Item A and your knowledge, evaluate the view that religion acts as a positive institution providing consensus in a society. (20 marks) **Spend 30 minutes on your response.**

HINTS TO HELP YOU RESPOND

This is a common question on the topic of beliefs and requires you to consider both sides of the debate. The item gives you a starting point for both your knowledge and counterargument; be sure to apply the correct perspective on the relevant side of the debate. Use functionalist views when discussing religion as a means to achieve consensus and Marxist views when citing religion as a source of class conflict.

Remember to be sure to define what is meant by consensus in your introduction and conclude with a balanced argument on whether religion can be viewed as positive or negative in a society. To highlight and back up your points you should also refer to a range of religions rather than just focusing on one particular faith.

Beliefs in Society: Religion's Impact on Changes in Society

For a long time there has been a debate in the sociological world about the impact religion can have on a society: Can it bring about mass social change or is it a tool to maintain the norm and retain traditional values? Many structuralists believe that religion acts as a conservative force, and that its role is to keep the morals and values of a society, while others cite religion as being instrumental in some of the biggest changes throughout history.

Religion as a Force for Change

In his book *The Protestant Ethic and the Spirit of Capitalism*, Max Weber identified how important a religion can be for social change. Weber studied Calvinists and he argued that their belief system was the start of early capitalism in the 16th century in northern Europe. Calvinists believed in **predestination**, that God had already selected a certain number of people who will get into heaven but no one knew if they were one of the selected few or not; Calvinists also believed that God's true will can never be known by humans, and that this causes what Weber terms **salvation panic,** the impossibility of knowing whether or not they will be saved. Hence, Calvinists observed a life of **asceticism** (living a pure and moral life) and worked hard to devote themselves to God, and believed that increased wealth was a sign of recognition from God that they would not receive the benefit of wealth if they were behaving wrongly. This encouraged Calvinists to continue to invest in more businesses and for Weber this provides evidence of the start of capitalism.

EVALUATION POINT

Although Weber shares an interest in capitalism and social class with Marxist theory, Marxists argue that the birth of capitalism can be traced to a variety of factors and not just Calvinism. Kautsky believed that the economic process of capitalism can be traced to pre-Calvinism, while other Marxists believe that true capitalism only emerged after the industrial revolution or advances in mass technology.

The Civil Rights Movement

In the 1950s, the civil rights movement began and Martin Luther King was one of the most iconic figures behind the campaign. The deconstruction of segregation by colour took a decade to begin, and Christianity played an important part in this change. Bruce notes that the Christian ideology of treating all men as equal was pivotal in the civil rights movement because it forced many White clergymen to question their personal values. Bruce observed that Martin Luther King referred frequently to Christianity in his speeches and concluded that religion can underpin huge social and political changes.

Memorial statue for Martin Luther King Jr. in West Potomac Park, Washington D.C.

Religion can be a force for positive political change as in the example of the civil rights movement. However, the new Christian right movement is more likely to try and maintain tradition rather than allow society to change. For example, many Christian movements are opposed to gay marriage, abortion and divorce.

The Liberation Movement

The liberation movement took place in Latin America in the late 1960s. Its aim was to try and help those in poverty, and it fought against many of the dictatorships in place. The Marxist sociologist Maduro stated that this movement is a classic example of religion inspiring social change; previously, the catholic church had adopted a conservative stance but liberation theology encouraged it to take a more left-wing approach to help those in need.

Although it was successful to an extent, liberation theology was only temporary and by the 1980s had come to a finish. It could therefore be argued that although religion can act as a force for change, more often than not it is halted rather than continuing to progress. Other Marxist views see religion only acting as a conservative force, which prevents revolution and change in society.

Millenarian Movements

Also known as **millenarianism**, the main purpose of these religious groups is to cause a major transformation of society; this is a concept that is common in many religions. According to the sociologist Worsley, these movements often focus on poverty and the saving of people due to belief in the second coming of Christ. Such movements could be found across Europe and the Western Pacific and they often influenced uprisings and the overthrowing of colonial governments.

Millenarian movements often achieved their aim, but it could be argued that these movements were political rather than religious, especially as many of them had predicted the second coming of Christ and a world of utopia free from pain and suffering, and of course it is argued that this has not happened. Christian missionaries ended up holding political power due to the promise of revolutionising standards of living for the poor.

SUMMARY

- Many theorists believe that religion can be a cause for social change, while others believe it acts as a conservative force.

- Weber believed that the Calvinist faith was the catalyst for the start of capitalism in northern Europe.

- The civil rights movement under Martin Luther King was driven by his Christianity.

- Bruce and Maduro both believe that religion can have a significant impact on social change.

- The liberation movement took place in Latin America and was influenced by the catholic church as a way to reduce poverty.

- The millenarian movement focused on the saviour of all people from an unfair world.

- Many of these movements are relatively short-lived rather than continuing to progress.

- Many Marxists and feminists believe that religion acts conservatively rather than as an instrument of social change.

QUICK TEST

1. What is meant by social change?

2. What is meant by predestination?

3. What is meant by the term asceticism?

4. Who led the civil rights movement in the 1950s?

5. Whereabouts did the liberation theology take place?

6. In what decade did the liberation theology take place?

7. Which type of religion was the driving force behind the liberation theology?

8. What is meant by millenarianism?

9. Which sociologist studied the overthrow of colonial governments during millenarian movements?

10. Which sociological perspectives tend to see religion as a conservative force?

PRACTICE QUESTION

Item A

Many sociologists believe that religion has had a huge impact on the progression of social change on societies. Weber believed that the start of capitalism can be traced back directly to a particular religious group and their beliefs.

However, other theorists believe that religion is more limited in the role it can play in advancing social change; indeed, many argue that religion is more likely to uphold tradition than actually change it.

Question 1: Applying material from Item A and your knowledge, evaluate the view that religion can be an instrumental force in social change. (20 marks) **Spend 30 minutes on your response.**

HINTS TO HELP YOU RESPOND

This question requires you to think carefully about both sides of the debate and if religion brings social change or whether it maintains the norm. It is important that you include a range of examples from around the world and back up your points with sociological theory. Ensure you include the phrase, 'conservative force' in your counterarguments.

Remember that Marxists are split on this argument; some argue that religion can be a force for change, while others argue that religion regulates the norm and maintains hegemony.

Beliefs in Society: The Secularisation Debate

Wilson describes secularisation as a 'process whereby religious thinking, practice and institutions lose social significance'. It is difficult to judge whether secularisation is occurring based on any one factor and therefore it is often placed into one of three categories: practice, thinking and institutions. What is certainly notable is that the extent of secularisation differs from country to country, and it is far more likely to be found in Europe than in the Middle East or Africa.

The Decrease of Religion in Practice

The simplest way to judge the decrease in the practice of religion is to look at attendance figures in places of worship. Sociologists such as Laslett (2016) have identified that the numbers attending church continue to fall: as many as a million fewer people currently attend church on a Sunday compared to 20 years ago. Many people have moved away from traditional religions to **spirituality**, or in some cases away from religion altogether. In Britain today shopping and live sport on a Sunday are common when in the past they were not permitted on Sundays, the day of rest. The census and social attitudes surveys show that almost 50 per cent of the British public now hold no religious affiliation at all; this can be seen as evidence of a process of what Weber called **disenchantment**, in which people seek out more rational explanations for events, instead of accepting events as simply the act of a supernatural power.

The Decline in Religious Thinking

Comte predicted that science was the final stage of human development and would eventually bring the end to religious thinking. Weber agreed that religion, magic and myth would be replaced by technology and bureaucracy through a process of **rationalisation**. Atheists such as Richard Dawkins and Sam Harris note that religious thinking has been replaced by rational thought and scientific evidence, and they believe that while science is based on **empirical evidence**, religion relies on the less valid element of blind faith. Postmodernists also agree with the decrease in religious thinking; Bauman argues that a religious vacuum has been left as people turn their back on religious ideas about creation. Lyotard supports this by stating that there has been a **breakdown of the meta-narratives**, that people no longer turn to religious stories as explanations for the world. Many societies are left with **religious pluralism** (the belief in two or more religions or an acceptance of more than one religious practice) rather than an expectancy to follow just one major faith; this has increased with the growth of religious movements and awareness of the alternatives that are available to individuals.

Some sociologists believe that religious pluralism is not evidence of secularisation but evidence that religious thinking changes over time (rather than people abandoning religion entirely). Others believe that religion and science can work in unison and that scientific discoveries often support points written in religious texts such as the Quran. For example, some Christians believe that God is the originator of the Big Bang.

The Loss of Power in Religious Institutions

Weber predicted that religion would be less of a force in society over time; with the development of science, religion became less sacred – he called this **desacrilisation.** The influence religion has in politics, education, and on the state has decreased over time. Bruce argues that many of the functions the church once had in society have been taken over by other institutions such as schools or the media. Berger notes that there is increasing religious diversity, and that the power of single institutions or faiths has decreased; for example, in the Middle Ages the catholic church enjoyed near total control but this single belief system eventually fragmented. Postmodern theorists such as Bauman also believe that **globalisation** has an impact on the influence of a single faith dominating an entire society; as people from different cultures mix, the strength that a dominant religion holds is diminished.

The functionalist Parsons accepts that the church has lost some of its functions but argues that religion still plays a significant role in the lives of many individuals and societies. Although the loss of the power of religion is noticeable in some parts of the world, in areas such as the Middle East it still plays a major role in politics.

Measuring Secularisation

It is difficult to measure the full extent of secularisation because religion is practised in different ways in different societies, and religion is often privatised as well, with many individuals having an individual relationship with God rather than a public expression of their faith. Others have an affiliation to a religion through socialisation or family but this does not necessarily identify them as being religious. There is also an increase in people that identify themselves as **agnostic** (the belief that God cannot be proven or disproven); it is difficult to categorise agnostics as they can neither be considered religious or not religious.

The study of secularisation tends to focus on religiosity in Europe and North America, and ignores the fact that religion still plays a significant role in other parts of the world. It should also be noted that there has been a recent rise in fundamentalism in some parts of the world, for example ISIS misconstruing the teachings of Islam and the rise of the Christian Right in the USA.

SUMMARY

- Secularisation can be measured through practice, thinking and institutional influence.
- Church attendances, social surveys and census statistics all indicate there has been a disenchantment and move away from religion.
- Weber predicted that rationalisation and developments in science would eventually see an end to the following of religions.
- Lyotard believes there has been a breakdown of the meta-narratives.
- Bauman argues that religious pluralism is further evidence of the process of secularisation.
- Weber stated that there has been a process of desacralisation and a decrease in the power held by religious organisations.
- Postmodernists believe that globalisation, development and economic growth lead to secularisation.
- It is difficult to measure the full extent of secularisation because religion has become more privatised and fragmented.
- Secularisation is only occurring in some parts of the world and it is not a universal process.

QUICK TEST

1. In which ways can secularisation be measured?
2. What did Weber mean by the term disenchantment?
3. What is meant by the process of rationalisation?
4. What do scientists mean by empirical evidence?
5. Explain an example of a meta-narrative?
6. What is meant by religious pluralism?
7. What is meant by desacralisation?
8. Which sociological perspective states that religion has been impacted by globalisation?
9. What is meant by agnosticism?
10. Where in the world is secularisation taking place?

PRACTICE QUESTION

Question 1: Outline and explain two ways in which science can be seen to have replaced religion. (10 marks) **Spend 15 minutes on your response.**

HINTS TO HELP YOU RESPOND

You need to make sure that your response has two very different examples and each one is of equal length. Remember that scientists believe they have the advantage of empirical evidence and you should aim to include this term and demonstrate your understanding of it. You could discuss the increase in rational thinking (Dawkins, for instance) and also Weber's desacrilisation.

Item A

In the Middle Ages, the catholic church had almost complete power and dominance over the lives of individuals in some parts of Europe. The church was pivotal in the role of the government as well as in education, family life, and in the rules, laws and regulations of a society. However, the period of reformation meant that the power faith held gradually lost significance over a period of time.

Question 2: Applying material from Item A, analyse two arguments in support of the idea that religions have lost many of the functions in society they once had. (10 marks) **Spend 15 minutes on your response.**

HINTS TO HELP YOU RESPOND

This question requires you to make use of and reference Item A, which looks at the loss of influence of the catholic church. The item notes some of the functions that catholicism used to exert power and therefore two examples can be pulled from the item and expanded upon.

It is important to incorporate key terms (for instance, secularisation, disenchantment) to back up your ideas and reference a range of sociologists. Remember that this question requires you to analyse and so you should also include counterarguments and evaluative points.

Beliefs in Society: New Forms of Religion and the Position of Religion Today

Previously, following a religion was an obligation and in many societies there was a punishment for not following its faith. In contemporary societies there has been a change towards individualism, choice and consumerism. Davie uses evidence to show that individuals now have more choice over religion and practice than at any previous point in history.

Religious Consumption and Spiritual Shopping

Davie (2007) believes that how people consume religion has changed and has become privatised, more of a choice than an obligation; for example, she points out how many people now believe without belonging, that although they have faith they are not an active member of a religious organisation. Voas and Crockett (2005) disagree with this argument and claim that a sizable number of people neither have faith nor belong to a religious organisation. Bruce agrees and claims that people don't have the time or inclination to devote themselves to a religion in the postmodern world. Hervieu-Legar (2006) says that a key feature of religious practice today is **spiritual shopping**, in which people choose aspects from a range of religions to suit their own needs and interests: this is called **pic 'n' mix religion,** 'do-it-yourself beliefs' or religious pluralism. The option of choosing from religions is a sign that increased secularisation is taking place in society.

EVALUATION POINT

Although an increase in the freedom of choice may be evident in some societies, in many parts of the world following a particular religion is still very much an obligation. For example, in some Islamic countries there are punishments for apostasy (abandoning religious belief and principles).

Spirituality Replacing Religion

In the late 1960s there was movement away from traditional religions towards spirituality; this was termed the **new age movement** in which interest grew in practices such as rebirthing, iridology and crystal healing. The Kendal project study in northern England identified an increasing number of people moving away from traditional Christianity and a growing alternative interest in **holistic spirituality**. According to the postmodernist Lyon, one of the key differences between spiritual practices when compared to mainstream religions is that they require less of a commitment, and that they are individualised to meet the needs of each person; they can be picked up, sampled and discarded as and when the user wishes.

EVALUATION POINT

Writers such as Glendinning and Bruce doubt the extent of the new age movement, and argue that the numbers who practice these on a regular basis are small and that their interest in such practices is often short-lived. Bruce also argues that many of those who follow a new age movement do not see it as a religious practice but either as a hobby or an avenue to good health and wellbeing.

The Religious Market Theory in Religion Today

Stark and Bainbridge oppose the secularisation theory and claim that religion is not in decline but has adapted and changed over time; while some faiths have declined in popularity others have experienced a revival through a process they call the **cycle of renewal**. They argue that religion fulfils many human needs and that people are naturally religious, so even though some religions fall out of popularity they are then replaced by newer or **revived faiths**. The researcher Finke has identified Buddhism in Japan, Evangelicalism in South Korea and the Hare Krishna movement in the USA as examples of beliefs that become global in the free market of religion. This theory proposes that faiths are actually more varied and globalised rather than fading away completely as proposed by the secularisation theory. The idea that there is now more choice suggests that there is an increased interest in religion.

EVALUATION POINT

Norris and Inglehart criticise the religious market theory because it ignores parts of the world where major faiths still have a monopoly, for instance the catholic church in South America. Beckford disagrees that people are naturally religious or need religion, and that this is not necessarily true for every individual.

The Changing Face of Religion and the Media

In a world of **media saturation** (a society in which lives are dominated by the media) religion has adapted to meet the demands of today. Helland (2013) has observed an increase in cyber religion which provides users with 24/7 access to practise their faith as well as online forums where they can discuss ideology. Hoover argues that people are going online to complement church attendance and not just as an alternative. Hadden and Shupe note how the increase in **televangelism** in the USA is another example of how religion adapts to oblige a media-influenced public.

EVALUATION POINT

Some postmodernists believe that the move towards online and television-based practice of faiths weakens the traditional ideas of many religions and is a step towards secularisation.

The Global View of Religion Today

It is difficult to judge levels of religiosity globally because countries can be so different from each other. In general, though, developed countries with strong economies tend to display declining levels of religious practice, where in poorer, more unstable countries the levels of religious practice remain high. Norris and Inglehart call this the **existential security theory**, in which levels of stability and survival rates have a direct link on the level of religious practice in each society.

EVALUATION POINT

It could be argued that the existential security theory is inaccurate when applied to the USA, which, despite being one of the richest countries in the world, displays high levels of religiosity, with fundamental Christian beliefs remaining strong and rising in several states. However, this phenomenon could be explained by the gap between the rich and poor in the USA.

SUMMARY

- Davie believes people have more choice over faith rather than following through obligation.
- There has been an increase in spiritual shopping or religious pluralism.
- The new age movement, or rise in spirituality, has replaced religion in some places.
- Bruce doubts the true extent of new age movements as a religious movement.
- Stark and Bainbridge note the rise of the religious market theory.
- Several religions have adapted to the increasing demands of the media in the world today.
- Norris and Inglehart refer to the existential security theory which states that the stability levels of a country affect its levels of religiosity.
- Postmodernists believe that these changes to religious practice are further evidence of secularisation.

QUICK TEST

1. What is meant by spiritual shopping?
2. What is meant by apostasy?
3. What is meant by pic 'n' mix religion?
4. Give two examples of new age practices.
5. Why do new age movements have less commitment than mainstream religion?
6. What is meant by the cycle of renewal?
7. What is meant by revived faiths?
8. What is meant by media saturation?
9. Which sociologists note the rise of televangelism?
10. Which sociologists introduced the idea of existential security theory?

PRACTICE QUESTIONS

Question 1: Outline and explain two ways in which new age movements differ to mainstream religion. (10 marks) **Spend 15 minutes on your response.**

HINTS TO HELP YOU RESPOND
You need to make sure that your response has two very different examples and each one is of equal length. It would be best to refer to a different new age movement in each of your two points and also refer to different types of religion in your answer. You should also aim to reference sociologists in each of your points.

Item A
In the postmodern world, religions have had to adapt to changes in the lifestyles of individuals and the development of mass technology, and many religions now offer a variety of ways to practise faith. However, many traditional religious practices have been retained and are still key elements today.

Question 2: Applying material from Item A and your knowledge, evaluate the view that religions are practised in a vastly different way today compared to 50 years ago. (20 marks) **Spend 30 minutes on your response.**

HINTS TO HELP YOU RESPOND
The question requires you to discuss a range of different religions, practices and developments and therefore your response should not simply focus on Christianity. It would be beneficial to structure your answer chronologically so you could begin by looking at the changes that started 50 years ago and continue to the more contemporary changes we see today.

To develop AO2 and AO3 skills you can discuss as to whether these changes in religion contribute to the secularisation debate; some believe that this is evidence that religion is adapting and changing, while others argue this is evidence of a weakening and decline.

Beliefs in Society: Religion and Globalisation

Globalisation refers to the interconnectedness of societies. Sociologists are divided on whether it has caused a decline or rise in religion, or has simply changed it. As noted in the chapter on 'Beliefs in Society: New Forms of Religion and the Position of Religion', religion has been impacted upon by the media, resulting in a rise in online religion and televangelism. Constant access to religion has caused people to question their own faith and to learn about other faiths; it can also strengthen their affiliations to some religions.

Globalisation and Secularisation

An analysis of countries becoming more secular can be linked to globalisation: as a religion loses its power and significance in one country, a similar pattern is often observed in neighbouring countries. For example, the spread of secularisation can be seen throughout northern Europe and the Scandinavian countries in particular. The popularity of **atheism** (the belief that there is not enough evidence to prove the existence of gods) can be linked to globalised media as people now have access to websites, documentaries and literature that may not have been previously available; for example, the theory of evolution may have been inaccessible in some religious educational environments, but there is now access to it via global media channels.

EVALUATION POINT

Secularisation can result in a counter-reaction in the form of fundamentalism; some religions see secularisation as an attack on faith and this can increase the strength of a religion in the form of a defence mechanism. Functionalists may see this creating a panic, which in turn reinforces the collective conscience.

The Rise of Fundamentalism

Fundamentalism in religion refers to those that observe a traditional and often literal interpretation of religious texts and doctrines; fundamental religions tend to oppose any group that challenges their interpretations of texts. It is not a surprise that fundamentalism has increased in response to the secular movement. One example of this is attitudes towards gender; according to Hawley, many fundamentalist groups believe in traditional female social and economic roles. This is in contrast to the feminist movement, which views these roles as **patriarchal** and reinforcing female oppression.

EVALUATION POINT

Fundamentalist groups have been criticised for using modern technology such as social media to spread their beliefs. This use of modern technologies could ultimately act as a threat to their fundamentalist views by impacting negatively on the religion's traditional core beliefs.

Reasons for the Rise in Fundamentalism

Davie believes that fundamentalist groups develop when they feel under threat from other faiths or secularisation; Castells calls this **resistance identity**. Similarly, Giddens suggests that fundamentalism is a reaction to changes in globalised countries such as the UK where abortion and gay marriage have been legalised and sex before marriage accepted; some fundamentalist groups identify these changes as being the key reasons for the breakdown of society and loss of its core values. Fundamentalists remain **dogmatic** (believing unwaveringly in a faith) and feel that these changes are creating an unstable and immoral world.

Beckford argues that many theories relating to the rise of fundamentalism are too simplistic and that some religions have adapted to changes in society rather than reverting to fundamentalism. One such example is the catholic church, which has recently relaxed its views on both homosexuality and female roles, with Pope Francis considering women as deacons.

Where Does Fundamentalism Develop?

According to Bruce, fundamentalism develops in religions that are **monotheistic** (faiths that believe in a singular deity) such as Judaism, Christianity and Islam. Bruce believes this is because the doctrines and texts of these faiths advocate the view that they are the only true and literal word of God. Therefore, because in monotheistic religions the true word of God must be followed, fundamentalists believe that those who don't follow these laws are committing sins. One example of this is Islamic fundamentalist groups such as ISIS that disagree with the behavior and values of the western world.

As well as religious fundamentalism, Davie believes that there has also been secular fundamentalism from the 1970s onwards due to increasing concerns about globalisation, the environment, and other risks to society.

Religion in a Global World

Globalisation has caused a split between those who wish to maintain religious traditions and those who wish for a secular world in which religious views are regarded as **antiquated**; this split has caused an increasingly unstable world and has become a major source of conflict. One example of this is ISIS (also known as ISIL, the Islamic State of Iraq and the Levant), a militant **jihadist** group that is responsible for a series of attacks across the western world and its own territories on those who fail to follow their particular brand of Sunni Islam. This has led many postmodern sociologists to argue that we are now living it what Beck calls a **risk society**, in which global links have caused new threats that societies must be aware of.

Horrie and Chippindale argue that it is important to not see Islam in its entirety as a threat to the western world; they state that fundamentalist groups like ISIS only consist of a small fraction of the world's 1.6 billion Muslims.

SUMMARY

- Globalisation has led to a split between secularisation and fundamentalism.
- Globalisation has caused secularisation and the rise of atheism to spread throughout many parts of Europe.
- Fundamentalism takes a traditional and literal interpretation of religious texts and doctrines.
- Fundamentalism is often a reaction to changes in society, and this is known as cultural resistance.
- Beckford observes that some religions do adapt to cultural changes rather than becoming more fundamentalist.
- Bruce identifies that fundamentalism is found within religions that are monotheistic.
- Davie states that there has been both religious and secular fundamentalism.
- The globalisation of religion has resulted in many conflicts and an increased risk society.

QUICK TEST

1. Where in the world is the spread of secularisation most common?
2. What is meant by an atheist?
3. What is meant by religion being patriarchal?
4. Which sociologist discusses the idea of resistance identity?
5. What is meant by the term dogmatic?
6. State two examples of monotheistic religions.
7. Which sociologist stated fundamentalism is related to monotheistic religions?
8. What is meant by the term antiquated?
9. What is meant by a jihadist?
10. Which sociologist discusses the ideas of a risk society?

PRACTICE QUESTIONS

Question 1: Outline and explain two ways in which fundamentalist beliefs can be viewed as patriarchal. (10 marks) **Spend 15 minutes on your response.**

HINTS TO HELP YOU RESPOND

This question requires you to combine your knowledge on fundamentalism and feminism; remember that there are different types of feminism and so discussing different examples of feminist viewpoints would be beneficial, for instance Hawley's Marxist feminist view. You could also discuss Giddens and the changes in society that are often a reaction to fundamentalism, for example changes relating to the legislation of abortion. You should define patriarchy fully and ensure your two examples are different and contrasting. Also remember that you will gain extra marks for the use of key terms and by referencing sociologists to back up the points you are making.

Item A

Many postmodernists believe that we are increasingly living in a risk society, and that one such reason for this is due to the religious conflicts that dominate our news; it would appear that these issues are growing in frequency and severity. However, some commentators believe that religious conflicts are nothing new, and that the evidence shows they have occurred throughout history and across a range of different faiths and countries.

Question 2: Applying material from Item A, analyse two arguments in support of the idea that globalisation will continue to cause religious conflict around the world. (10 marks). **Spend 15 minutes on your response.**

HINTS TO HELP YOU RESPOND

This question requires you to make use of and reference the item, which gives you some useful starting points for constructing your two arguments. Remember that you are looking to consider two different examples so it would be an advantage to not base your entire response on one particular religion; using contemporary examples could also be of benefit in your answer.

Remember that this is an analysis question and so strong critical analysis and counterarguments are required; you should reference sociologists to back up the points you are making.

Beliefs in Society: Types of Religious Organisation

Although the number of religious groups and organisations around the world is vast, sociologists categorise them by placing each in one of four types: churches, sects, denominations and cults. There are also new age movements but these are often seen as spiritual rather than religious. The differences between religious groups can be defined in terms of size and commitment although many go through changes at various stages in their history and can therefore be placed in different categories at different times.

Churches

According to the sociologist Troeltsch a church is a large established religious organisation with a rigid structure and hierarchy. Examples of these are the Church of England and the Roman Catholic church, both of which have close connections to the state and also claim to have a **monopoly over the truth** (a belief that a particular faith contains the true messages and ideas). Because of their size, churches are usually integrated into mainstream society, are followed by large numbers, and are often the official or national faith of a particular country.

EVALUATION POINT

Bruce argues that due to both religious pluralism and the increase in atheism, the monopoly of power that religions such as the Church of England once had is now on the decline.

Sects

According to Troeltsch, sects are the opposite to churches because they are small with no complex hierarchy; they are often in direct opposition to mainstream society. Examples include Calvinism, the People's Temple Agricultural Project (Jonestown) and Branch Davidians; they are groups with extreme beliefs who frequently dedicate themselves to these sects due to dissatisfaction with mainstream religion or the outside world in general. Sects often appeal to those who are **marginalised** by society and act as a saviour from their own personal deprivation or issues.

EVALUATION POINT

In the media, cults and sects are often muddled up; based on Troeltsch's categorisation, examples such as Jonestown are definitely sects.

Although there is no complex hierarchy, there is invariably a strong and charismatic leader driving the group.

Denominations

Denominations are distinct from churches in that they do not have such large numbers of followers and loyalty is usually not as strong. Toeltsch adds that denominations do not claim to have a monopoly on the truth; if they have a hierarchy it is not complex and they are not as closely linked to the state in the same way that churches are. Baptists and modern day Methodists are examples of denominations.

EVALUATION POINT

Denominations are usually splinter groups from mainstream religions. Many commentators suggest that denominations are more tolerant towards other religious organisations in comparison to church organisations.

Cults

Cults are usually led by a practitioner. They do not demand a strong commitment in the same way that sects do, and they are usually held together with no firm structured hierarchy. Bruce defined cults as movements without a fixed set of beliefs, where the focus is on inner power, individuality and mysticism. Cults are difficult to define; Mormons and Jehovah's Witnesses are frequently referred to as examples of cults.

EVALUATION POINT

Many of the more extreme groups are sects rather than cults. The media refer to cult followings and cult groups in sociological terms. Cult groups are less likely to be as extreme and dangerous as sects.

New Religious Movements

New religious movements (NRMs) is a blanket term for the many new religions and organisations that grew in popularity during the 1960s. Wallis suggests that there are three different types of NRMs:

1. World-rejecting NRMs such as the Moonies or the Children of God. The focus of these groups is the rejection of the outside world and an attempt to achieve salvation; they are likely to isolate themselves from other communities and often end in fatal circumstances.
2. World-accommodating NRMs are usually splinter groups from a main religion; this is invariably because the group has become disillusioned with the way the main religion is heading and so they seek to restore purity in their faith by breaking away. Examples include the Neo-Pentecostalists, who split from mainstream Catholicism.
3. World-affirming NRMs who in principle accept the world as it is but hope to improve life for its followers by overcoming issues such as unhappiness, relationship problems, unemployment and illness. Perhaps the best known example is Scientology.

EVALUATION POINT

Some sociologists such as Stark and Bainbridge criticise Wallis' categorisation of NRMs, claiming they are too diverse and complex to be categorised so simply. Many religions are difficult to categorise due to disagreements over their status.

New Age Movements

New age movements (NAMs) is a blanket term for a range of practices including crystal healing, astrology and meditation. Heelas proposes that there are somewhere in the region of 2,000 such activities in the UK; these have become increasingly popular in the last 40 years. Heelas suggests that there are two different types of NAMs:

1. Self spirituality NAMs which focus attention away from religion to look at the self.
2. **Detraditionalisation** NAMs which seek to learn from personal experience rather than relying on the word of a priest or rabbi.

Drane believes that many of those who turn to NAMs do so because they have become **disillusioned** with mainstream religion.

EVALUATION POINT

Some sociologists such as Bruce do not recognise NAMs as religious organisations; indeed, many of the followers of the NAMs do not regard their practices as religious, for them a NAM is no more than a hobby.

SUMMARY

- Religious groups can be categorised into churches, sects, denominations and cults.
- Troeltsch labels groups based on commitment, hierarchy, size and links to the state.
- Sects are usually the most extreme groups but are often incorrectly referred to as cults.
- Denominations are often splinter groups who have broken off from mainstream religions.
- Cults tend to be small, loosely knitted together groups without a fixed set of beliefs.
- Wallis defines new religious movements as either world-rejecting, world-accommodating or world-affirming.
- There are a vast number of new age movements that began to gain popularity in the 1960s.
- Many sociologists reject NAMs as a form of religion or as religious organisations.

QUICK TEST

1. What are the four types of religious groups?

2. Which sociologist defined these different categories?

3. What is meant by the term marginalised?

4. What is meant by the monopoly of truth?

5. Baptists would be an example of what type of group?

6. The Mormons would be an example of what type of group?

7. What do we call groups that isolate themselves from the outside world?

8. What is meant by detraditionalisation?

9. What is meant by the term disillusionment?

10. Give an example of a sociologist that does not believe that NAMs are religious organisations.

PRACTICE QUESTION

Item A

New religious movements began to emerge in the 1960s and by the end of the decade there was a huge number of these groups. Sociologists have tried to explain why these groups gained popularity and examined issues such as the movement away from mainstream religions.

However, other theorists believe that the vast majority of these groups are relatively short-lived and the reputation of such movements has been clouded by the way in which they came to an end.

Question 1: Applying material from Item A and your knowledge, evaluate different sociological explanations for the emergence of New Religious Movements. (20 marks) **Spend 30 minutes on your response.**

HINTS TO HELP YOU RESPOND

This question asks you to look at NRMs as a whole and therefore there is an opportunity to discuss a range of such practices including cults and sects. Remember not to confuse NRMs with NAMs as this is a common mistake made by sociology candidates. You should be looking to include several examples of NRM groups throughout the essay.

The question also enables you to consider the characteristics of people who joined such groups and so you can make synoptic links to knowledge in relation to gender, age, social class and ethnicity; remember that many of these groups appealed directly to particular types of people. This question also expects you to be able to apply sociological theories such as Marxism and postmodernism.

Beliefs in Society: Religious Ideology and Scientific Thinking

There has been a long-running debate regarding science and religion and whether the two can complement each other or whether they contradict each other. The debate also raises the question of whether science and religion are in search of absolute truth or are simply belief systems.

Science may have made huge progress in recent times but whether it has replaced religion is open to debate.

Science and Objectivity

The evolutionary biologist Richard Dawkins believes that (unlike religion) science deploys **objectivity and empiricism**. Dawkins notes that science remains objective but religion relies on faith in texts that were written a long time ago. By empiricism he means that science is evidence-based, that conclusions are drawn from observable experience, and are not just **preconceived ideas**. Dawkins believes that science is an **open system** in that it continues to test, reassess and develop over time as new scientific discoveries are made.

Evolutionary biologist Richard Dawkins believes that science deploys objectivity and empiricism.

Lynch argues that science is not always as objective as it thinks, that scientists often work with a clear hypothesis and structure their experiments to try and meet their pre-conceived ideas. Some theorists even argue that science is simply replacing the function of religion.

Sociology as a Science

Positivist or structuralist sociologists believe that sociology can be viewed as a science by adopting the same methodologies as the scientific world. Theorists such as Comte and Durkheim applied the **inductive approach** to research by constructing a hypothesis, testing the hypothesis, then repeating their research through to reliability and forming a conclusion. This approach to research aimed to apply scientific research methods to reach conclusions regarding social behaviour.

Anti-positivists (interpretivists) believe that scientific methods cannot be used on humans in the same way that they can be used for studying chemicals; humans have free will and therefore their behaviour is much less predictable than the behaviour of atoms or chemicals. They argue that science is no better than religion in explaining human behaviour.

Popper and the Falsification Theory

Popper agrees that science is an open belief system in which science is constantly open to change and the subsequent updating of current theories. Popper refers to this as **falsification** in that scientists should be continually looking to falsify and disprove theories in an attempt to improve them. Popper uses the **black swan theory** as an example of this and thus avoiding making the assumption that all swans are white. Popper advocates the deductive approach (as opposed to the inductive approach) and argues ideas should be flashes of inspiration, which can come from anywhere, with investigation taking place afterwards.

EVALUATION POINT

Gomm argues that science is not always as open as claimed because it is related to social context. Gomm contends that scientists are not keen to falsify their own theories but tend to work towards proving their own hypotheses and rejecting findings that are contrary to their own beliefs. This encourages debate, suggesting that science could be more flawed than religion.

Kuhn and the Paradigm Theory

Kuhn believes that science is more of a **closed system** than portrayed because scientists work within restrictions or guidelines he calls **paradigms**. He argues that scientists working within a particular framework or ideology look for accepted ideas that fit it and that it takes a huge amount of evidence before there can be a **paradigm shift** or a scientific revolution. His contention is supported by Polyani who observed the tendency towards a **circularity of beliefs** in the scientific world, in which the majority develop theories that match expectancies to avoid changing existing belief systems. Therefore the scientific paradigm can be seen as a closed belief system.

EVALUATION POINT

Scientists respond that if science was a closed system then no new scientific discoveries would be made, and that developments are continually taking place due to the open nature of scientific research.

Mannheim's Theory of Ideology and Utopia

Mannheim believes that all theories, beliefs and religions have a one-sided perspective and contain an element of bias. He identifies belief systems based on **ideological thought** that seek to protect the interests of the privileged, examples being systems of capitalism or patriarchy, which maintain clear levels of hierarchy. The other type of belief system is **utopian thought**, which advocates social change for the underprivileged and offers a vision of a more equal world. An example of a utopian thought system is Marxism, which advocates communism as an alternative to capitalism. Each belief system is only a partial truth of the world.

EVALUATION POINT

Mannheim identifies two very clear and distinct thought processes; however, his theory has been criticised because it would be impossible to create a society that can incorporate both of these alternative viewpoints.

SUMMARY

● There is debate about whether science and religion can coexist or if they contradict each other.

● Dawkins believes science has the benefit of objectivity and empiricism and that religion does not.

● Positivists believe that sociology can be a science by employing the same methodologies as the world of scientific research.

● Popper believes science is an open system that continually aims to falsify theories and beliefs.

● Popper refers to the black swan theory as an example of how the scientific model should function.

● Gomm argues that scientists always work within a particular social construct.

● Kuhn believes that most scientists operate in closed systems and paradigms.

● Polyani argues that scientists tend to work in the circularity of belief style system.

● Mannheim states that belief systems fall into either ideological or utopian thoughts.

QUICK TEST

1. What is meant by the term objectivity?

2. What is meant by empirical evidence?

3. Which group of sociologists believe that sociology is a science?

4. What is meant by the inductive approach to research?

5. What is meant by falsification?

6. Which theorist introduced the black swan theory?

7. What is meant by a closed belief system?

8. What is meant by the term paradigm?

9. Who introduced ideas on the circularity of beliefs?

10. What are the two thought belief systems according to Mannheim?

PRACTICE QUESTIONS

Question 1: Outline and explain two ways in which science can be deemed as more objective than religion. (10 marks) **Spend 15 minutes on your response.**

HINTS TO HELP YOU RESPOND

To answer this question you need to start by defining clearly what is meant by objectivity; you then need to construct two arguments that are quite different from each other; you could discuss Durkheim's use of inductive logic and also Dawkin's stance on objectivity. You should reference key sociologists and also develop ideas in relation to empirical evidence. You need to divide your answer equally between the two arguments.

Item A

Many scientists work within a particular area of specialism and therefore aim to prove their theories and hypotheses are correct; critics suggest that this causes their findings to be socially constructed or biased (this is referred to as a closed system of beliefs).

However, many theorists suggest that if science were not open to new ideas then the scientific world would stay stagnant and never develop, advance or improve.

Question 2: Applying material from Item A, analyse two arguments in support of the idea that science works within a closed system of beliefs. (10 marks) **Spend 15 minutes on your response.**

HINTS TO HELP YOU RESPOND

This question requires you to dedicate an equal amount of time to each argument; within those points you should include terms such as social construct, paradigm and circularity of beliefs. Key writers such as Kuhn and his view of the scientific paradigm should be applied to back up your points.

Remember you need to provide a counter-argument and use analysis as well. Positivism, empiricism, open systems and objectivity can all be explored in your answer.

Crime and Deviance: Functionalist Theories, Subcultural and Strain Theories

Functionalists believe society is like a human body, it consists of a number of different systems all required for the smooth running of society as a whole; they call this **organic analogy**. In order for society to operate harmoniously its members must share norms, values and beliefs; this is known as **value consensus**. Society must perform the role of **socialisation**, essentially instilling the shared values in its members so that they know how to behave. It must also provide **social control** by providing positive sanctions for behaviour that conforms to the value consensus and negative sanctions for behaviour that is considered deviant.

Crime

Key functionalist Emile Durkheim (1893) stated that crime was a healthy part of every society. He suggests that crime is both **universal and inevitable**, meaning that it will occur in every society no matter what. In every society some people will naturally be inadequately socialised and **anomie** (normlessness: a sense of not knowing what is expected in society) will exist as people and groups become more diverse and disconnected from the value consensus.

EVALUATION POINT

In modern society the existence of one set of shared values can be questioned. However, the concept of criminals straying from the norms of society is supported by sociologists such as Hirschi, who stated that crimes occur when an individual's bonds of attachment to society are weakened.

Crime and Deviance

Durkheim sees crime and deviance as serving two important functions for society. Firstly, crime ensures **boundary maintenance**. By punishing individuals who commit crime other members of society are shown that the offender's behaviour is unacceptable, reinforcing a sense of **social solidarity**. Secondly, deviance is often the start of **adaptation** in society. For society to progress, the existing norms must be regularly challenged and this can, in turn, lead to social change.

EVALUATION POINT

Durkheim fails to state how much crime is inevitable and healthy for society. It could be argued that if society needs crime to achieve social solidarity, its key functions are not operating effectively.

Deviant Behaviour

Strain theories suggest that deviant behaviour occurs when individuals are unable to achieve society's shared goals by legitimate means. Robert Merton (1938) believes that two factors lead to crime: **structural factors**, which make opportunities in society unequal and **cultural factors**, which make individuals focus solely on the goals of society and not necessarily on how to achieve them. Merton focused on the American Dream of financial success and noted the legitimate ways in which Americans are meant to achieve this (through education and work).

Merton argues that an individual's opportunities are affected by society's unequal structure (like poverty) and the increasing cultural pressure to be wealthy. He states that a strain forms between the goal of financial success and the legitimate means of achieving this.

There are a number of ways in which people can respond to this strain, and that reaction is often a reflection of the individual's position in society. **Innovation** is the response of an individual who accepts the goal of financial success yet seeks illegitimate (often illegal) ways of achieving this goal. **Conformity** is when a person simply continues to aim for the approved goals by the legitimate means. **Ritualism** occurs when an individual loses sight of the goal yet continues to work in a legitimate environment simply following the rules. **Rebellion** occurs when individuals find their own new goals and ways of changing society (for example, cults). **Retreatism** is when an individual rejects the legitimate goals, means and values of society, possibly reverting to drug or alcohol misuse.

EVALUATION POINT

Marxists would propose that Merton fails to acknowledge the ability of the ruling class to create laws that restrict the ability of the working class to follow legitimate ways of achieving financial success, and that he also fails to explain crimes committed by those who do not experience strain in society. Despite this Merton does support Durkheim's concept of anomie occurring when the values of society become weak and fail to prevent its members from behaving deviantly. Rosenfeld and Messner (2001) support Merton with their recent strain theory, stating that in the USA the most valued goal is financial success. Subcultural strain theories argue that deviance is created within subcultures that provide a focus other than financial success.

Non-Utilitarian Crime

Albert Cohen (1955) supports Merton's concept of the increasing culture of financial success, although he sees the reaction to this strain as a group response rather than that of an individual one. He also notes that not all crime is **utilitarian** (for financial gain). Merton fails to explain non-utilitarian crime such as vandalism, which is committed for financial reasons. Cohen stated that working-class boys find it harder to succeed in the middle-class education system when they face **status frustration**. The working-class boys rejected the values of the middle-class system and created their own alternative status hierarchy, which saw them gaining status through being deviant.

EVALUATION POINT

Cohen offers an explanation as to why non-utilitarian crime occurs, although his work is mainly focused on one social group and fails to examine other genders and social classes.

Subcultures

Cloward and Ohlin (1960) focus on the subcultural responses that occur as a result of the strain between legitimate goals and means in society. They believe there to be unequal access to the **illegitimate opportunity structure** in which criminal careers exist. Not everyone who experiences strain automatically responds with innovation. Different areas in society provide different illegitimate opportunity structures.

Criminal subcultures exist in areas where criminal role models provide a structure for youths to follow to become successful criminals. **Conflict subcultures** occur in societies that are unstable and do not allow for a criminal subculture to develop. Here, gang violence prevails, allowing a release from the frustration of strain. **Retreatist subcultures** develop when individuals fail in both the legitimate and illegitimate opportunity structure, and these groups will revert to alcohol or drug misuse.

EVALUATION POINT

Marxists see subcultures as a response to capitalism and would suggest that Cloward and Ohlin fail to explain the crimes of the rich and powerful; they focus too much on working-class crime. It may also be incorrect to suggest that an individual will solely follow the characteristics of one subculture, some may follow traits from more than one subculture. There may also be a suggestion that not all individuals and groups start out with the same goal of financial success.

SUMMARY

- Functionalists believe that society must provide effective socialisation and also social control for its members.

- Emile Durkheim stated that crime is inevitable and universal in all healthy societies. It performs boundary maintenance, reinforcing social solidarity, and also allows for adaptation in society.

- Merton's strain theory sees crime as a reaction to strain between legitimate goals and the legitimate means of achieving them in society.

- According to Merton there are five reactions to strain: innovation, conformity, ritualism, rebellion and retreatism.

- Albert Cohen suggests that crime is a subcultural response to status frustration for working-class boys. He explains that not all crime is utilitarian.

- Cloward and Ohlin note the three subcultures that people may have access to in the illegitimate opportunity structure: criminal subcultures, conflict subcultures and retreatist subcultures.

QUICK TEST

1. What is the process called in which norms and values are instilled in members of society?

2. According to Merton, what are the two factors in society that lead to crime?

3. What is meant by utilitarian crime?

4. According to Cloward and Ohlin, what occurs in a retreatist subculture?

5. Which term is given to the normlessness in society?

6. In Merton's responses to strain, which response would involve an individual creating their own illegitimate way of obtaining the goals of society?

7. According to Albert Cohen, what do working-class boys experience in the middle-class education system?

8. In Cloward and Ohlin's explanation of subcultural responses to strain, which response would involve fighting between rival gangs?

9. Which recent strain theorists support Merton in suggesting that financial success is the main goal in modern America?

10. Which members of society should experience positive sanctions according to functionalists?

PRACTICE QUESTIONS

Question 1: Outline two responses to the strain between legitimate goals and legitimate means in society. (4 marks). **Spend 6 minutes on your response.**

> **HINTS TO HELP YOU RESPOND**
> Select two of Merton's responses to strain here. Keep your notes brief with a quick explanation of each. Start each point on a new line. For example: Innovation means to seek out a new method of achieving society's goals, possibly through illegitimate means.

> **Item A**
> Subcultural strain theorists Cloward and Ohlin note that working-class youths are likely to be denied opportunities in the legitimate opportunity structure. They also suggest that opportunities in the illegitimate opportunity structure can also be restricted and access to different subcultures can determine how a working-class person responds to strain in society. Some areas are more likely to have criminal hierarchies than others; others may simply contain rival groups; and in other areas drugs and alcohol may be a crutch for those denied legitimate chances.

Question 2: Applying material from Item A, analyse two subcultural responses to strain. (10 marks) **Spend around 15 minutes on this response.**

> **HINTS TO HELP YOU RESPOND**
> Read Item A carefully and decide exactly which responses you will use. You must use content from Item A. So, because Item A discusses criminal hierarchies, you could mention criminal subcultures. You will also see links to conflict subcultures where Item A mentions rival groups or you could use the drugs and alcohol line to discuss retreatist subcultures. Make your points in two separate, detailed PEEEL paragraphs (PEEEL: make a Point, Evidence it, Explain it, Evaluate it and then Link it back to the question).
>
> For example: Cloward and Ohlin focus on the subcultural responses of working-class youths to the strain in society between legitimate goals and legitimate means of achieving them. They note that in different areas there are different subcultures that youths can access. As Item A states, some areas may have existing criminal hierarchies; in these areas a young person may become part of a criminal subculture. They may aim to gather experience in criminal activities from those with successful criminal careers above them, working their way up the criminal hierarchy in order to obtain wealth and the financial success goal of society. They do, however, fail to note that some subcultures may exist in which mainstream goals are not an objective. In the criminal subculture working-class youths will receive training in organised crime from professional criminals, allowing them to access the legitimate goals of society through illegitimate means.

Crime and Deviance: Labelling Theory

Labelling theory derives from interactionist sociologists who are interested in how acts can be seen as deviant. They see deviance as a **social construct**. Howard Becker (1963) noted that groups in society create a set of rules and apply them to others; he calls these people **moral entrepreneurs**. The people who they label as deviant become **outsiders**. They themselves, or the acts they do, only become deviant when labelled so by others.

Typifications

Labelling theorists suggest that certain groups are more likely than others to be labelled as deviant by agencies of social control. Reiner (1985) found that some police officers share a **canteen culture** that focuses on White, male, conservative values. In turn, police officers were more likely to stop and search ethnic minorities, labelling them as deviant. Cicourel (1976) found that police officers use **typifications** in stopping, arresting and charging individuals. These typifications are based on stereotypes about who is most likely to commit crime, meaning that working-class and youths from ethnic minorities are more likely to be arrested. Middle-class individuals are less likely to be charged.

EVALUATION POINT

The use of typifications by officers means that labelling theorists are likely to reject the validity of official statistics. Marxists reject the work of labelling theorists because they fail to examine where the initial labels caused by the inequality of the capitalist system came from. It fails to examine who made the rules in the first place (from their perspective: the ruling class).

Primary and Secondary Deviance

Edwin Lemert (1972) examined how labels can cause further deviance. He notes two stages of deviancy. **Primary deviance** is simply acts that go against the norms and values of society but have not yet been labelled by others. **Secondary deviance** occurs as a result of being labelled as deviant; this can have a dramatic impact on an individual, causing them to become an 'outsider' for example. The label may also become the individual's **master status**, defining them as a person and potentially perpetuating a career in deviance.

EVALUATION POINT

Individuals have the ability to reject their negative labels. It is not a certainty that once a label is applied to a person a self-fulfilling prophecy will occur. Downes and Rock (2003) suggest that individuals are able to choose how they respond to their label.

The Deviance Amplification Spiral

The application of a label to an individual may result in secondary deviance. Jock Young (1971) looked at how cannabis smokers were labelled. He noted that the police (and wider society) labelling the group as deviant caused them to form a deviant subculture in which their cannabis use was accepted. Cannabis use increased among the group as an instance of a **self-fulfilling prophecy**.

Attempts by social control agencies such as the police to stop deviance can lead to an increase in the deviance itself; this is known as the **deviance amplification spiral**.

Stanley Cohen (1972) wrote about how society's reaction to mods and rockers involved in small-scale scuffles at seaside resorts caused further deviance to occur. The media exaggerated the events, causing moral panic to spread across society. Moral entrepreneurs called for the police to tighten their control. The mods and rockers became **folk devils** demonised by society. This led to them becoming marginalised, resulting in further deviance.

EVALUATION POINT

Not all deviant acts are shamed in the same way. Braithwaite (1989) noted two types of shaming. Disintegrative shaming is when the act and the individual are labelled deviant. Reintegrative shaming is when the act is labelled deviant but the actor does not become stigmatised by their actions. This suggests that not all labelleing leads to a deviance amplification spiral or a self-fulfilling prophecy.

Mental Illness

Interactionists are also interested in the labelling of individuals as deviant in terms of mental illness. Many interactionists see statistics about mental illness as a social construct. Medical professionals have the capacity to attach labels of **mental illness** to individuals. Edwin Lemert (1962) studied **paranoia** in individuals. Some people naturally struggle to integrate into groups; this is an act of primary deviance. However, secondary deviance occurs when the individual excluded from the group is seen as an outsider or awkward. The individual may become more concerned that others are excluding them and in turn fear for their own mental health. Thus the paranoia will become a self-fulfilling prophecy.

EVALUATION POINT

Lemert's view fails to explain why the individual displayed the primary deviance of social awkwardness in the first place. The nature of interactionism failing to explain why original acts occurred in the first place can be seen as a criticism of the entire perspective.

Suicide

Emile Durkheim used the topic of **suicide** to promote sociology as a scientific discipline. He used official statistics to discover if suicide was the result of a person's levels of integration and regulation in society. This research has been rejected by interactionists as its positivist approach and reliance on official statistics means it lacks validity. Jack Douglas (1967) stated that suicide statistics are socially constructed and are simply the product of the interactions of the actors who define the death as a suicide (coroners, police officers and family members). Durkheim's view that a lack of integration can cause suicide can be argued against by Douglas' insight that a person who has a close family – who want to avoid believing that their relative took their own life – is less likely to have their death categorised as a suicide by the coroner.

Max Atkinson (1978) believes that the coroner uses **common sense knowledge** when deciding whether or not a death is a suicide. This means that the official statistics are simply a construct that reflect the individual views of the coroner.

EVALUATION POINT

It would be naive to reject all official statistics surrounding crime simply because they are constructed by individuals. Official statistics are highly useful in crime prevention and control.

SUMMARY

- Labelling theorists see deviance as a social construct. Moral entrepreneurs create deviance by labelling individuals and acts as deviant.

- Certain groups are more likely to be labelled deviant than others; the canteen culture of the police force and officers' use of typifications impact on official crime statistics.

- Primary deviance occurs when a deviant act is committed. Secondary deviance is a result of society's reaction to the deviant act.

- Labelling of groups as deviant can cause a self-fulfilling prophecy to occur.

- Clampdowns by control agencies can cause a deviance amplification spiral. Labelled groups become folk devils, marginalising them from society.

- Medical professionals have the ability to label someone as mentally ill. This can lead to the person questioning their mental health further.

- Interactionists see suicide statistics as social constructs, created by the interactions between actors around the deceased person.

- Coroners use their own commonsense knowledge to decide whether or not a death is a suicide.

QUICK TEST

1. Which sociologist originally looked into labelling in 1963?

2. According to Atkinson, what do coroners use when deciding whether or not a death is a suicide?

3. Which term does Becker use to describe individuals who label others and their acts as deviant?

4. Which groups became folk devils in Stanley Cohen's study *Folk Devils and Moral Panics*?

5. Which aspect of mental health did Edwin Lemert study?

6. What does a label become when it ends up defining a person?

7. What did Cicourel suggest police officers use when judging an individual?

8. What is the difference between primary and secondary deviance?

9. Which term describes the shared White, conservative views of the police force?

10. What did Downes and Rock suggest individuals have the ability to do with their label?

PRACTICE QUESTIONS

Item A

Labelling theorists are interested in how and why an individual or act becomes deviant. They see the process of creating deviance as a social construct, rather than examining why people are deviant in the first place. Labelling theorists are interactionists who look closely at the processes of interactions between individuals and how this impacts on their behaviour. Labelling theorists look at how the label of deviant can cause individuals to become further isolated from society, potentially creating further deviant behaviour.

Question 1: Applying material from Item A and your knowledge, evaluate the usefulness of labelling theory as an explanation for crime and deviance. (30 marks) **Spend 45 minutes on this response.**

HINTS TO HELP YOU RESPOND

Start with an explanation of labelling theory, reference Howard Becker and ensure you explain the concept of moral entrepreneurs labelling acts and individuals; link this to Item A by using language such as '…as in Item A…'. Examine the use of labels in police actions from the canteen culture through to the use of officers' typifications. Reference Edwin Lemert to explain the importance of the reaction to labelling and question this using Downes and Rock. Explain how secondary deviance can be caused by media reactions using Stanley Cohen's example of mods and rockers. Question the ability to reject a negative label referencing Braithwaite. Throughout your response use other theories to contrast your points. Strain theories can be used to suggest that labels are unimportant; it is simply the pressure of achieving goals legitimately that causes crime and deviance. Use Marxist views to explain how labels may be applied to some groups rather than others, yet labelling theory fails to establish the origins of these labels.

Question 2: Outline two advantages of labelling theory. (4 marks) **Spend 6 minutes on this response.**

HINTS TO HELP YOU RESPOND

Keep it short and precise. Start each point on a new line. You can use advantages such as the theory of looking at individuals in depth rather than groups in society. You could discuss the ability to look at the impact individuals have on others in terms of their deviant or criminal behaviour. For example: One advantage of the labelling theory is that it allows a person to see the impact of society's reactions to a person's behaviour on their future acts. It allows us to question the impact of labels on the act of secondary deviance.

Crime and Deviance: Marxist Theories of Crime

Traditional Marxism looks at a capitalist society where the **bourgeoisie** (ruling class) exploit the **proletariat** (working class) for profit. Marxism agrees with the labelling theory that states certain groups in society are treated unfairly in comparison to others. They examine how the structure of society ensures that the interests of the bourgeoisie are served, from law creation to the criminal justice system.

Traditional Marxism

Traditional Marxists propose that the nature of capitalism causes crime to occur; they call capitalism **criminogenic** as it breeds crime in all social classes. The working class are likely to commit crime for a number of reasons. Naturally, due to **exploitation** by the ruling class, the working class will experience poverty and crime may simply be a means of survival. Advertising promotes material goods that the working class are less likely to afford, so may feel a sense of **relative deprivation**, turning to crime to obtain these goods. Non-utilitarian crimes may also be committed by the working class simply out of frustration at the inequality of the capitalist system.

EVALUATION POINT

Traditional Marxism can be considered as too deterministic. Simply being a member of the working class does not mean that a person will commit crime. Even some of the most isolated individuals living in extreme poverty choose not to commit crime.

The Ruling Class

Capitalism is also criminogenic for the ruling class. Capitalism promotes the acquisition of wealth and property. In a competitive environment members of the ruling class may turn to criminal activities to secure further wealth. Official crime statistics often fail to highlight these ruling-class crimes as the law is selectively created and enforced. Marxists acknowledge that those who create laws are members of the ruling class themselves, and as a result of this those laws protect the ruling class. Lauren Snider (1993) argues that corporate crimes committed by the ruling class hurt more individuals than working-class crime; she notes that the ruling class also avoid passing laws that could make it difficult for businesses to make a profit.

EVALUATION POINT

Snider's argument supports that of labelling theorists who note the inequality of treatment of individuals by social control agencies such as the police.

False Consciousness

Marxists argue that a few laws passed to support the working class are merely a tactic used to lull them into a **false consciousness**. Frank Pearce (1976) notes that the laws passed to support the health and safety of workers also benefit the ruling class as they help keep the workforce healthy and thus ensure that they are able to continue wage-slaving to provide profits for the bourgeoisie. These laws promote the caring face of capitalism.

EVALUATION POINT

Traditional Marxism fails to note the impact of structural forces outside of social class, for example ethnicity and gender. Also, despite health and safety regulations being ignored by businesses, there have been occasions on which corporations have faced significant repercussions at the hands of the criminal justice system.

The Voluntaristic View of Crime

Neo-Marxists take a **voluntaristic** view of crime. They combine the views of traditional Marxism with those of labelling theory. Taylor, Walton and Young (1973) agree with traditional Marxists that capitalism is criminogenic. They also agree that the state is controlled by the ruling class and in turn makes laws that support the bourgeoisie. However, they see the traditional Marxist view of crime as too deterministic. They state that crime is a choice, consciously undertaken by the criminal, sometimes with a political motive to fight the capitalist system. Criminals are not simply acting passively; they are actively trying to change society. Taylor, Walton and Young claim that several factors need to be taken into account to gain a full social theory of deviance, combining what the act means to the individual committing it (from labelling theory) and the structural causes of the act (inequality highlighted by Marxism).

EVALUATION POINT

Taylor, Walton and Young fail to note the impact of crime committed by the working class on other members of the working class. They take a glamorised view that all crime is politically motivated and aimed at changing society. Positivist sociologists also state that crime statistics can be accurate and relevant.

White Collar Crime

The criminogenic nature of capitalism causes **white collar crime** to occur. This includes **corporate crime** – committed by employees for the benefit of a company, and also **occupational crime** – committed by employees for their own personal benefit. Tombs and Whyte (2015) note that corporations are constructed through law and politics in ways that impel them to cause harm to people and the environment. They suggest that corporate crime is a widespread and deeply rooted problem, meaning that businesses should be more strictly regulated.

Professionals who are members of the ruling class hold a powerful position over the working class. Members of the working class must place **trust** in them, with their health, money and environment. These professionals are able to abuse this level of trust to exploit the working class. For example, Dr Harold Shipman, a GP who is believed to have murdered over 200 of his patients over 23 years in practice. Corporate crime and the abuse of trust is often hidden due to the media and law courts focusing more on other social classes and areas of society.

Corporate crime may occur as a result of **differential association**, where employees are socialised into the criminal ways of the company and are able to dismiss their deviant behaviour as simply following instructions. Companies may become weary of following legitimate means to obtain wealth and end up seeking illegitimate methods, which are more lucrative.

EVALUATION POINT

The Marxist view of corporate crime assumes that all companies are unscrupulous and would act deviantly if they were able to avoid legal restrictions. There are many ethically sound organisations that would disagree with this. Also, the view that capitalism spurs crime through competition for wealth fails to explain the crimes of non-profit organisations such as the police, or non-utilitarian white collar crimes, such as those of Harold Shipman.

SUMMARY

- Marxists highlight the inequality in capitalist society. They are concerned with the exploitation of the proletariat by the bourgeoisie.

- Traditional Marxists see capitalism as criminogenic, causing crime in all social classes.

- Law creation is focused on protecting the ruling class as the bourgeoisie create laws.

- Laws passed to protect the working class are merely a display of the caring face of capitalism and have an agenda to support the ruling class.

- Neo-Marxists take a more voluntaristic view of crime, combining aspects of traditional Marxism and labelling theory.

- Criminogenic capitalism promotes white collar crime, including corporate and occupational crime.

- Ruling-class professionals have the ability to exploit members of the working class due to the level of trust placed in them.

- There are many reasons why corporate crime may occur, it may be a result of differential association or due to the search for more lucrative ways of securing wealth.

QUICK TEST

1. What are the two classes in society according to traditional Marxists?

2. What do Taylor, Walton and Young aim to discover by looking at a range of factors?

3. Which main theory combines traditional Marxism in the neo-Marxist view of crime?

4. According to Marxists, what do laws to protect the working class create?

5. Why might traditional Marxism be considered as too deterministic?

6. Which GP exploited their power and trust in order to murder over 200 patients?

7. Which term is used to describe employees being socialised into criminal activities that are embedded into the workplace?

8. Which type of laws does Lauren Snider claim the ruling class are reluctant to pass?

9. What might advertising in the capitalist system cause among the working class?

10. What does the statement that capitalism is criminogenic mean?

PRACTICE QUESTIONS

Item A
Traditional Marxism is concerned with the class divide in society between the bourgeoisie and the proletariat. Traditional Marxists see crime as a reaction by the working class to their exploited position in society; they also note that ruling-class crime occurs because the capitalist system encourages unscrupulous competition in which criminal activity becomes embedded.

Neo-Marxists agree with traditional Marxism in considering society to be based on a significant level of inequality; however, they see crime as an active choice made by the individual.

Question 1: Applying material from Item A and your knowledge, evaluate the Marxist perspective of crime and deviance. (30 marks) **Spend around 45 minutes on this response.**

HINTS TO HELP YOU RESPOND
Start by explaining the basic view of Marxism and the concept of a criminogenic capitalist system. Note the existence of working-class crime due to poverty and relative deprivation. Discuss ruling- class crime as a result of unscrupulous competition and link this to Item A. You can add clarity to this by explaining why occupational and corporate crimes may occur. Evaluate this along with non-utilitarian occupational crimes such as Harold Shipman's.

Explain that the traditional view is too deterministic. Use neo-Marxism to contrast this and explain Taylor, Walton and Young's full social theory of deviance. Evaluate this with the view that it romanticises crime as an act to change society. Also aim to evaluate by using contrasting theoretical viewpoints (for instance conflicting views of Marxism contrasted with the consensus views of functionalism).

Question 2: Outline two reasons why white collar and corporate crime occur. (4 marks) **Spend around 6 minutes on this response.**

HINTS TO HELP YOU RESPOND
You should aim to explain differential association and also the concept of illegitimate means being an attractive proposition to acquire more wealth. Start each point on a new line. For example: Corporate crime may occur as legitimate ways of obtaining wealth for the company are less lucrative than illegitimate ways. Companies may ignore health and safety regulations in order to maximise profits.

Crime and Deviance: Realism and Crime

Realist sociologists are different to Marxists and labelling theorists as they see crime as a real problem which needs to be tackled rather than a simple social construct; they accept official statistics as accurate and useful. Realist views are split politically into two camps, left realism and right realism.

Right Realism

Right realism comes from a New Right **conservative perspective** and rejects the idea that crime is a result of inequality in society. Left realism links with Marxism and questions the structural causes of crime.

Right realists see crime as a growing problem and are focused on solutions to crime. They see structural explanations of crime (such as Marxism) as being too lenient on the criminal. Right realism suggests practical solutions to crime which mainly focus on **tough punishments** as opposed to tackling poverty.

The causes of crime for right realists are the result of three main factors:

Rational Choice Theory – Clarke and Cornish (1986) observe that human beings have free will over their actions. They suggest that all actions are the result of rational choices made by the actor. In making a rational choice about crime, the rewards of the crime are weighed up against the risks of the crime. For example, a high monetary reward may outweigh the risk of a significant prison sentence. Right realists are concerned that the crime rate is high because the perceived cost of crime is too low, and as a result they state that punishments need to be tougher.

EVALUATION POINT

If crime is simply a result of a rational choice, why do patterns of crime suggest some social groups are better at choosing not to commit crime than others? Right realists also suggest that crime may be a result of biological differences in individuals and poor socialisation; if so, then these factors may reduce an individual's ability to think rationally about crime.

Biological Differences – Wilson and Herrnstein (1985) propose a biosocial view of crime. They see crime as a combination of biological factors that make some individuals more likely to commit crime; examples of these are **aggressive personality traits**, low levels of intelligence, low control over impulses, and also social factors.

EVALUATION POINT

There are issues with suggesting that criminals are likely to be of low intelligence. Many criminals choose a lucrative criminal career in the illegitimate opportunity structure that requires a high level of intelligence and a distinct skill-set.

The Rise in the Underclass – Charles Murray (1990) argues that the decline in the effectiveness of the family to teach core values and self-control has resulted in the creation of an underclass. Traits that define the underclass include welfare dependency and a lack of desire to undertake paid work in the labour market, dependency on drugs or alcohol and a rise in illegitimate children raised without a male role model. Murray sees this group growing as a result of the generous welfare provisions made by the state. The underclass finds crime an accepted method of acquiring wealth.

EVALUATION POINT

The underclass may not be a choice, it may be the result of the unequal distribution of wealth in society as highlighted by Marxists.

Right Realist Solutions to Crime

Right realist solutions to crime focus on control and punishment. Wilson and Kelling (1982) noted that areas in which crime has noticeably taken hold are more likely to be hotspots for criminal activity. For example, an area that has high levels of graffiti and vandalism is likely to encourage further crime. They suggest that programmes created to immediately repair and address these issues demonstrate that criminal behaviour is not tolerated and thus reduce crime; this is known as **broken windows theory**. Right realists also suggest that police should control local areas by adopting a **zero-tolerance** approach to crime. Because they see crime as a result of a rational choice, right realists also suggest that **target hardening** should take place, during which the perceived costs of crime are increased; this situational crime prevention may take the form of increased CCTV or more locks on doors.

EVALUATION POINT

Right realism ignores the structural causes of crime such as poverty. It also focuses too heavily on street crimes, failing to note corporate and occupational crime.

Left Realism

Left realists focus on inequalities in society although they differ from Marxists as they believe a revolution is not the answer, but rather a smooth and gradual change in society. They reject traditional Marxism because it fails to examine the impact of working-class crime.

Left realists believe that victims of crime are likely to be members of groups that are disadvantaged by the inequalities in society, such as working-class individuals or members of minority ethnic groups. These individuals are likely to be failed by the police who fail to investigate racist attacks and domestic violence.

Lea and Young (1984) are key left realists and note that there are three factors that cause crime to occur:

Relative Deprivation – caused by the advertisement of consumer goods in the capitalist system. This helps explains the increase in crime as living standards have risen in a number of western societies. Relative deprivation means that a person feels deprived in comparison to those around them.

Subculture – subcultures develop among groups who experience relative deprivation. These subcultures share their own unique set of values and may in turn accept criminal behaviour.

EVALUATION POINT

You can support this with Cloward and Ohlin's notes about criminal subcultures located within the chapter on 'Crime and Deviance: Functionalist Theories, Subcultural and Strain Theories'. However, it fails to explain why some individuals who experience relative deprivation seek out subcultures and others do not.

Marginalisation

Marginalisation – left realists notice that some groups are more likely to be marginalised in society than others. Unemployed young people who feel a sense that they are not supported in society are likely to become disconnected from society's values. This may result in frustration and non-utilitarian crimes such as vandalism.

Left realism's solutions to crime focus on **democratic policing**, in which the police and the public work together, enabling the public to take ownership of policing decisions and processes. They also favour a range of social controls, for example the use of social services and improved housing projects. Left realists focus on tackling the inequalities in society at its roots. Provision of jobs and housing can be one method of reducing inequality and in turn reducing crime. Left realists see the value in the community policing itself.

EVALUATION POINT

Left and right realist approaches naturally act as effective evaluation points of each other, one rejecting inequality as a cause of crime and the other seeing it as the main catalyst for crime. Functionalist views can be used to support right realism and Marxism naturally supports left realist views about inequalities in society.

SUMMARY

- Realist sociologists criticise other theories of crime as they fail to offer an effective solution.

- Right realism is a conservative political perspective that focuses on control and punishment as solutions to crime.

- Clarke and Cornish (right realists) believe that crime is a result of a rational choice and that in order to prevent crime from occurring the risks must far outweigh the rewards.

- Biological differences are to blame for crime according to right realists Wilson and Herrnstein.

- Charles Murray suggests that the growth in crime rates are a result of a growth in the underclass.

- Right realist solutions to crime include target hardening, zero-tolerance policing and broken windows theory.

- Left realists see crime more as a result of inequalities in society. They believe that relative deprivation causes crime.

- Groups that experience relative deprivation are likely to become marginalised according to left realists. These marginalised individuals may then fall into deviant subcultures.

- Left realists favour solutions to crime that tackle its root causes, such as improvements in housing and job availability. They also promote democratic policing.

QUICK TEST

1. Which right realist believed a growth in the underclass to be a cause for the rising crime rate?

2. What is the name of the left realist theory that suggests areas should be kept in a good state of repair to prevent crime from taking root?

3. What type of policing is preferred by left realists?

4. Which political perspective does right realism come from?

5. What do Wilson and Herrnstein suggest is a key factor in causing crime?

6. What is meant by the term rational choice theory?

7. Which term describes the feeling of not having what those around you have?

8. What types of crimes might frustration over marginalisation lead to?

9. What term is used when the perceived costs of crime are increased?

10. Which realist perspective would attribute poverty in society as a main cause of crime?

PRACTICE QUESTIONS

Item A

Right realists see crime as a real issue in society. They believe that crime needs an effective solution and should not be tolerated. Right realism suggests that crime may be the result of lifestyle choices made by individuals or inadequate socialisation. Right realists suggest that crime can be tackled by reducing the rewards of criminal behaviour and by taking a zero-tolerance approach to policing.

Other sociologists argue that right realists fail to acknowledge the structural causes of crime.

Question 1: Applying material from Item A and your own knowledge, evaluate the usefulness of the right realist approach to crime and deviance. (30 marks) **Spend 45 minutes on this response.**

HINTS TO HELP YOU RESPOND

Start by explaining the basic background of right realism and its roots in conservative thinking. Continue to explain the right realist causes of crime from rational choice theory through to biological differences and the rise in the underclass. Evaluate these causes as you explain them by using left realist views suggesting that right realism fails to note the structural causes of crime and that it focuses too heavily on working-class crime. You can also use Marxist explanations of crime and the prevalence of corporate and occupational crime. Continue to explain solutions to crime from the broken windows theory to zero-tolerance policing; again, evaluate if these are merely focused on working-class crime and thus fail to tackle the root causes of crime that left realists note or ruling-class crime as Marxists note.

Question 2: Outline two left realist causes of crime. (4 marks) **Spend 6 minutes on this response.**

HINTS TO HELP YOU RESPOND

Start each point on a new line. Select two from relative deprivation, subcultures and marginalisation. For example: Marginalisation may cause many people to commit crimes as they feel rejected from society, causing them to act against the shared values of society and turn to crime.

Crime and Deviance: Crime and Gender

Official crime statistics show that women are under-represented at all stages of the criminal justice system. In 2013, women made up 18% of the population arrested, 25% of all criminal convictions, and 5% of the prison population. These statistics suggest males commit more crime. Sociologists question the validity of the statistics and consider why men may commit more crime, why women are less likely to be criminals, and whether or not women simply evade punishment.

Chivalry Thesis

Otto Pollak (1950) suggests that the criminal justice system acts more leniently towards women. He reasons that this is because the criminal justice system consists predominantly of men, from those working in court to police officers. Pollak believes that women are less likely to be convicted of crimes because potential criminal charges are often dismissed by men in the criminal justice system acting leniently. He calls this the **chivalry thesis**.

EVALUATION POINT

Chivalry thesis is supported by Flood-Page *et al*'s (2000) examination of self-report studies; they found that 14% self-reported male offenders had been cautioned or prosecuted; in comparison only 9% self-reported female offenders had faced a caution or prosecution.

However, Steven Box (1981) found that when serious criminal offences were examined, women were not treated more leniently than men. Buckle and Farrington (1984) found that in some crimes, for example shoplifting, women were more likely to be prosecuted than men. It is also evident that women who do not fit society's feminine stereotypes are likely to face harsher sentences.

Class and Gender Deals

Pat Carlen (1988) used Hirschi's theory of control to explain that female crime occurs as a result of class and gender deals. Carlen argues that working-class women are offered two potential deals in society. The **class deal** is when women are able to work for a living and thus achieve a satisfactory lifestyle. The **gender deal** is when women are able to take a traditional domestic role in the family and thus gain the emotional rewards of a satisfactory family life. Carlen studied 39 working-class women who had been convicted of a range of crimes; she found that many had experienced setbacks in the class deal, being rejected for job vacancies and struggling to access the welfare state. She also found that many of these women had also been denied the gender deal since they had experienced turbulent family lives. Carlen concluded that when nothing is to be gained from either deal, there is nothing to be lost if a crime is committed.

EVALUATION POINT

A study that comprises only 39 individuals cannot be considered comprehensively representative. Carlen's view is, however, supported by many feminists as it highlights the failures of a patriarchal society.

Functionalist Sex Role Theory

Functionalist sex role theory focuses on how female crime rates could be low because of **socialisation**. Talcott Parsons (1955) examined the role of women in the family home. Parsons found that at home women take on the **expressive role** and are in charge of socialising the children into the norms and values of society. Parsons believes that girls will be socialised more effectively by their mother than boys will, because with boys their father takes on the instrumental role – boys wish to take on this role also and reject the expressive role of their mother. Albert Cohen (1955) examined crime among working-class boys, and he noted that many turned to a criminal lifestyle as a result of the absence of a **male role model.**

Liberation Thesis

Freda Adler (1975) examined the changing status of women in society. Adler's **liberation thesis** proposed that as a decline in **patriarchal society** takes place women become more liberated from its constraints. This liberation of women leads to female offending matching that committed by males; female opportunities for committing crimes have increased while controls preventing female crime occurring have decreased. The nature of female crime has also evolved because of this, and that with more women in higher positions in the business world there are more opportunities for those women to commit white-collar crimes.

Patriarchal Control and Masculinity

Heidensohn (1985) believed the rate of female offences was lower than male offences because of the **patriarchal control** women face in society. He noted that women are controlled at home, work and in public. At home women are controlled by the duties of their domestic role and the threat of violence existing in the relationship they have with their male partner. Daughters are controlled by the restrictions placed on them. Girls at home are expected to carry out domestic chores and as part of a bedroom culture are encouraged to socialise with peers at home rather than walk the streets.

Many sociologists have studied why men are more likely to offend than women. It is evident from the official statistics that the majority of criminals have always been male.

James Messerschmidt (1993) focuses on the concept of **masculinity**. He observes males as having to accomplish their masculinity in society. He notes that some males are at a natural advantage over others when accomplishing their masculinity because they have access to the financial resources required. **Hegemonic masculinity** is the predominant type of masculinity in society, favoured by the majority of men. It is obtained through work in the paid labour market, is outwardly heterosexual, and includes the capacity to subordinate women. Some men have **subordinated masculinities** because they lack the necessary financial resources to accomplish hegemonic masculinity. These may include men from a lower class and/or ethnic minorities; some of these men may turn to crime to accomplish their masculinity. Males with access to corporate occupational crime opportunities may use these to achieve their hegemonic masculinity.

SUMMARY

- Official statistics suggest that significantly more males commit crime than females.

- Otto Pollak suggests that the criminal justice system treats females more leniently than males and that this explains the difference in the statistics. This is called chivalry thesis.

- Pat Carlen suggests that females turn to crime when they are denied either the class deal or the gender deal in society.

- Functionalist sex role theory notes that females commit less crime due to their socialisation and the expressive role that they take on in the family.

- Freda Adler argues that female crime is on the rise as a result of liberation from the constraints of patriarchal society.

- Patriarchal control can be blamed for the significant gap in offending between genders. Heidensohn argues that women are controlled at home, at work and in public.

- Male crime can be explained by the aim of accomplishing masculinity. Messerschmidt suggests that not all men are able to achieve hegemonic masculinity, and that some men who have subordinated masculinities may turn to crime.

QUICK TEST

1. Which sociologist suggested that crime occurs due to subordinated masculinities?

2. According to Heidensohn, where are women controlled?

3. In 2013, what percentage of the prison population in the UK was female?

4. According to Talcott Parsons, what role do women take on in the family causing them to be less likely to commit crime?

5. What is the most dominant and preferred type of masculinity in society?

6. Which crime did Buckle and Farrington look at where women were more likely to be prosecuted than men?

7. What were women able to do when offered a class deal in society?

8. What does Albert Cohen suggest is a cause of male crime?

9. Which theory does Otto Pollak offer for the difference in rates of offending shown in crime statistics?

10. What type of culture is promoted among young girls, which makes them less likely to turn to crime?

PRACTICE QUESTIONS

Item A

Official statistics suggest that females commit significantly less crime than males. A number of sociological theories offer an explanation for this pattern. Some functionalist sociologists suggest that women are socialised differently to men and that this impacts on their likeliness to commit crime. Others argue that patriarchal society restricts a woman's opportunity for committing crime. Some theorists simply use an explanation of the desire to be seen as masculine in society as a reason for the higher number of male offences.

Question 1: Applying material from Item A, analyse two reasons why crime statistics display a significantly higher proportion of males committing crime than females. (10 marks) **Spend 15 minutes on this response.**

HINTS TO HELP YOU RESPOND

You must use Item A here. There are three significant causes that you can select from within it: functionalist sex role theory, patriarchal control, and also accomplishing masculinity. Select two to discuss. Your points should be in two detailed PEEEL paragraphs (make a Point, Evidence it, Explain it, Evaluate it, and then Link it back to the question). For example: As Item A states, some sociologists 'suggest that women are socialised differently to men', these include Talcott Parsons who discussed the functionalist sex role theory, which explains why women commit less crime than men. Women are socialised into an expressive role within the family, they in turn are in charge of socialising the children of the family into the norms and values of society. Young girls respond to the socialisation provided by their mothers more effectively and as a result are less likely to turn to crime than their male siblings

Question 2: Outline two causes of male offending. (4 marks) **Spend 6 minutes on this response.**

HINTS TO HELP YOU RESPOND

Start each of your points on a separate line. You can select from a number of causes, although you may want to use Messerschmidt's accomplishing masculinity and Cohen's lack of a male role model. Keep your points brief. For example: James Messerschmidt suggests that males are more likely to commit crime as they are pressurised to accomplish masculinity. Some men experience subordinated masculinity as a result of their social class and in turn use crime to become masculine.

Crime and Deviance: Crime and Ethnicity

Official statistics show that Black, Asian and minority ethnic groups are more likely to be over-represented in the criminal justice system than those from a White ethnic group. The 2011/2012 crime statistics for England and Wales showed that a person from a Black ethnic group was six times more likely to be **stopped and searched** by the police than a person from a White ethnic group. A Black person was nearly three times more likely than a White person to be **arrested**. When sentenced, Black, Asian and minority ethnic groups received a larger proportion of immediate **custodial sentences** compared with the White ethnic group.

Ethnicity of Offenders

The **Crime Survey for England and Wales** (CSEW) is a **victim survey** that asks respondents to record details of crimes they have experienced in the last year. When discussing the ethnicity of offenders, respondents are likely to identify offenders as members of Black, Asian or minority ethnic groups. Members of ethnic minority groups are also more likely to be the victims of crimes.

EVALUATION POINT

Self-report studies ask respondents to anonymously declare their own criminal actions. Graham and Bowling (1995) found that when self-reporting crime, individuals from both White ethnic groups and Black ethnic groups had a similar rate of offending. This suggests that there may be issues with the representativeness and validity of official crime statistics and victim surveys.

The Criminal Justice System

The **criminal justice system** (CJS) is a complex series of stages. To fully understand the possible reasons behind differing levels of offending across ethnic groups, processes within the CJS must be examined thoroughly. The **Macpherson report**, launched

as a result of the failings of the police to properly investigate the racist murder of Stephen Lawrence in 1999, found the police service to be **institutionally racist**. Stuart Hall (1978) describes how the police demonise Black groups to justify military style policing. Bowling (1999) states that police often behave in a racially prejudiced way, resenting ethnic minorities who live in what were once traditionally White areas.

EVALUATION POINT

Many studies observe how police officers communicate with each other 'backstage', when off the streets. However, these results do not prove that the values shared by officers when backstage are reflected in their working practices.

Ethnic Minority Offending

Left realists suggest that ethnic differences in crime statistics reflect a real issue of ethnic minority offending. Lea and Young (1993) see crime as a result of the **relative deprivation** experienced by many ethnic minority groups, due to which these groups may become **marginalised** in society and form deviant **subcultures**. High levels of unemployment among young Black males can lead to **utilitarian crimes** such as theft. Lea and Young believe that institutional racism in the CJS cannot be solely to blame for the differences in offending rates.

EVALUATION POINT

The vast majority of crimes tackled by the police are a result of members of the public raising concerns. This suggests that the statistics cannot be a pure reflection of police attitudes.

The Myth of Black Criminality

Neo-Marxists argue that Black criminality is a social construct resulting from racist stereotypes. Paul Gilroy notes the **myth of Black criminality** and claims that African-Caribbean groups and Asians are no more criminal than other ethnic groups but are recorded so heavily in crime statistics as a result of the racist stereotyping by the CJS. Gilroy believes ethnic minority crime is a display of political resistance against a racist society stemming from the poor treatment of ethnic minority groups at the hands of British imperialism (when the British Empire exerted oppressive rule over many other countries).

The neo-Marxist Stuart Hall examined the use of young Black males as a distraction from the **crisis of capitalism** taking place in the 1970s. A moral panic was created about Black muggers. Hall notes that at the time unemployment was high, that there was political unrest that led to strikes by workers.

Hall states that there was no real evidence of a rise in the crime of mugging committed by Black youths; he proposes that the moral panic acted as a scapegoat to distract the public from the crisis of capitalism. By creating a **folk devil** in Black youths, the working class was divided, preventing any chance of them weakening the capitalist system.

EVALUATION POINT

Downes and Rock (2011) disagree with Hall *et al* and state that Black street crime was rising throughout the 1970s as a result of the restricted job opportunities for young Black workers. Hall fails to explain exactly how the crisis created the moral panic.

The Legitimate Opportunity Structure

Philippe Bourgois (2000) examined the El Barrio area of New York, which was a Black and Hispanic community. Like Cloward and Ohlin (see page 33) he saw the crime committed by ethnic minorities as a result of restricted opportunities in the **legitimate opportunity structure**. He saw Black and Hispanic individuals as excluded from society who had to create their own ways to survive within an illegitimate opportunity structure, combining legal methods of obtaining money with illegal sidelines.

Ethnic minority groups are also more likely to become victims of crime in society. Police statistics from 2014/15 show over 54,000 racist incidents recorded. These are only the reported incidents; because they lack faith in the police force, individuals from many ethnic minority groups choose not to report their **victimisation**. Minorities often feel as though they are **over-policed** as a result of their local areas being patrolled heavily; they also feel **underprotected** by the police.

SUMMARY

- Official statistics suggest that Black, Asian and minority ethnic groups are more likely to commit criminal offences than members of White ethnic groups in society.

- Black, Asian and minority ethnic groups are more likely to be stopped and searched by the police, be arrested, and also receive custodial sentences.

- The Crime Survey for England and Wales is a victim survey that suggests individuals may use racial stereotypes when identifying an offender.

- The Macpherson report found the police service to be institutionally racist.

- Left realists suggest that ethnic minority groups are more likely to commit crime as they are likely to experience relative deprivation, marginalisation and form deviant subcultures.

- Neo-Marxist Paul Gilroy believes there to be a myth of Black criminality with ethnic minorities acting criminally to resist a racist society.

- Stuart Hall examined the moral panic related to young Black muggers and found that Black youths were used as a scapegoat to distract the public from a crisis of capitalism.

- Bourgois stated that Black and Hispanic inhabitants of El Barrio were excluded from the legitimate opportunity structure, forcing them to rely on criminal activities.

- Ethnic minority groups also face higher levels of victimisation.

QUICK TEST

1. Which report investigating institutional racism in the police force was launched following the death of Stephen Lawrence?

2. Which sociologists believe that the relative deprivation experienced by Black, Asian and minority ethnic groups is a major cause of minority crime?

3. Which sociologist studied El Barrio and the restricted access to legitimate opportunities faced by Hispanics there?

4. Which moral panic did Stuart Hall examine in the 1970s?

5. What does Paul Gilroy state about Black criminality?

6. How many racist incidents were recorded in police statistics in 2014/15?

7. In 2011/12 how many times more likely was a Black person to be arrested in comparison to a White person?

8. What did Stuart Hall believe Black youths were used to distract society from?

9. What issue is there with focusing heavily on observing police behaviour backstage?

10. Which sociologist believes ethnic minority crime to be a display of political resistance against a racist society?

PRACTICE QUESTIONS

Item A
Black, Asian and ethnic minority groups are over-represented in every stage of the criminal justice system. In 2011/12 ethnic minority groups were six times more likely to be stopped and searched by the police than Whites. Many sociologists suggest that this is due to institutional racism within the police force, others argue that this cannot explain the different rates of offending. Some sociologists suggest that ethnic minority groups are more likely to commit crime due to their position in society.

Question 1: Applying material from Item A and your own knowledge, evaluate the view that high rates of offending among ethnic minority groups are the result of institutional racism. (30 marks) **Spend 45 minutes on this response.**

HINTS TO HELP YOU RESPOND
You need to start by explaining the notion of institutional racism in the police force; use the Macpherson report in your explanation alongside Stuart Hall and Bowling to support the argument that this is the main cause of differing levels of offending in the official statistics. Use some statistics to display the extent of over-representation in all stages of the criminal justice system for ethnic minority groups. Link this to Item A and the statistics of higher rates of stop and search. You can also link this to labelling theory.

Use connectives that show you are evaluating, such as *in contrast to this*. Add conflicting arguments from left realism that show ethnic minority groups as more likely to offend. Add contrast from neo-Marxism by referencing Paul Gilroy. Use Philippe Bourgois explaining the denial of legitimate opportunities to link to Item A and the position in society of minority groups. Throughout your response ensure that each paragraph links effectively to the question.

Question 2: Outline three reasons why official statistics show ethnic minority groups as more likely to engage in criminal activities than White groups in society. (6 marks) **Spend 9 minutes on this response.**

HINTS TO HELP YOU RESPOND
Start each point on a new line. You can select any three explanations of the statistics from either inaccuracy in statistics due to institutional racism through to arguments suggesting ethnic minority groups to be more likely to offend.

Crime and Deviance: Crime and the Media

Fallacies About Crime

With a significant growth in the variety of media outputs in society, the impact of the media on crime via both fictional and non-fictional formats has become an area of important sociological debate. Although about 30 per cent of newspaper content covers crime, this is not in line with official crime statistics but can potentially change the readership's view of criminal activity. Marcus Felson (2002) notes how the media creates the following fallacies about crime:

- **Ingenuity fallacy** – the media shows criminals and detectives as intelligent; detectives need to be clever to solve crimes.
- **Age fallacy** – criminals and victims are shown mainly as adults, despite official statistics suggesting that they are predominately young.
- **Class fallacy** – victims are shown as mainly middle class, despite statistics suggesting that they will mainly come from working-class areas.
- **Victim fallacy** – media portrayals of victimisation highlight risks to the elderly and women. In reality, those living in poverty and minority ethnic groups are more likely to fall victim to crime.
- **Police fallacy** – police are shown to succeed in catching criminals and solving more crimes than is reflected in practice.
- **Dramatic fallacy** – everyday crimes are under-reported and violent crimes are over-reported. Sooth and Walby (1991) note that British newspapers are preoccupied with sex crimes, misrepresenting the reality of rape. They regularly show rapists as strangers rather than as people already known to the victims, which is who they are more likely to be.

EVALUATION POINT

Fallacies are impacted upon by news values. Cohen and Young (1973) state that news is **manufactured**: journalists must manufacture news that is worthy of the reader's attention, and this means that news is often a misrepresentation of official crime statistics. News is a **social construct**.

News Values

News values impact on a story's worthiness of being in the news. If the story meets any of the following values it is more likely to receive media attention:

- **Dramatisation** – showing action or excitement.
- **Personalisation** – stories that people can relate to, showing personal elements such as tragedy.
- **Higher status persons** – events involving celebrities or those with power in society.
- **Novelty or unexpectedness**.
- **Risk** – stories that show risk to the readership, making them feel vulnerable.
- **Bad news** – crime is mainly bad news. Media output tends to take the focus away from positive stories.

EVALUATION POINT

Since the media focuses on novel or unexpected events it naturally focuses on deviant actions as these are disconnected from the norms of society.

The Media

The media has been questioned as a cause of crime. One suggestion is that audiences may imitate violent actions as displayed in Bandura *et al*'s (1961) experiment in which children were shown as likely to imitate an aggressive role model when acting violently towards a **Bobo doll**. The media can cause arousal by showing violent or sexual imagery; it may also glamorise crime and transmit knowledge of criminal techniques.

Fear of Crime

By focusing on victimisation the media can often cause a **fear of crime**. Schlesinger and Tumber (1992) found that newspaper readers and those who watch large amounts of TV are more likely to be concerned about leaving home at night and falling victim to crime.

Relative Deprivation

Left realists Lea and Young (1996) state that the media creates a sense of **relative deprivation** among disadvantaged groups in society by stimulating a desire for consumer goods through advertising which they can't afford. This can result in **frustration** leading to utilitarian or non-utilitarian crimes to obtain these goods.

Moral Panics

Moral panics can be created by the media. Media attention can cause society to over-react in relation to a particular issue. The media has the capacity to identify certain groups in society as **folk devils**; negative media attention can cause further deviant behaviour in the group identified. **Moral entrepreneurs** voice their concerns about the behaviour of these groups and call for control

agencies to clamp down on behaviour by groups that they deem to be deviant. The labelling of groups as deviant can enable a **self-fulfilling prophecy** to occur, and this may result in deviance amplification. A crackdown on particular groups can cause them to be further stigmatised, resulting in a **deviance amplification spiral**.

In 1972 Stanley Cohen wrote *Folk Devils and Moral Panics,* which focused on how the media portrayed mods and rockers following clashes between the two groups in the 1960s (see also the chapter on 'Crime and Deviance: Labelling Theory'). He found that the media over-reacted to the events, **exaggerating and distorting** them with sensationalised headlines. The media also **predicted** further violence to take place, causing a heightened awareness and risk of future disturbances.

Cyber-crime

Rising rates of **cyber-crime** across global networks are a result of technological development. Policing cyber-crime is difficult because of the scale of the internet and the difficulty of monitoring users' internet browsing activity. The introduction of new media has led to changes in the way that crime is presented, with social media channels becoming alternatives to traditional news outlets.

SUMMARY

- The media misrepresents patterns of crime via a number of fallacies including misrepresentations about age, class and ingenuity.

- The news is manufactured as a social construct. Particular types of events are more likely to be reported in the news than others.

- News values include: dramatisation, personalisation, higher-status persons, novelty or unexpectedness, risk and bad news. Each of these factors make a particular event more likely to be reported as news.

- It has been suggested that the media cause crime through imitation.

- Focus on victimisation can lead to a fear of crime created by the media.

- Left realists suggest that media advertising causes a sense of relative deprivation in marginalised groups, resulting in utilitarian and non-utilitarian crimes.

- Moral panics created by the media highlight certain groups as folk devils. Mods and rockers were an example of this illustrated by Stanley Cohen.

- Once deviant groups are highlighted by the media, deviance amplification spirals may occur resulting in more deviant behaviour.

- There has been a growth in cyber-crime, which is difficult to police, as a result of changes in media outputs and the growth of new technologies.

QUICK TEST

1. Which sociologist wrote *Folk Devils and Moral Panics*?

2. What may occur as a result of a clampdown by control agencies following the media highlighting a group as deviant?

3. What impacts on a story's worthiness of appearing in the news?

4. Which groups were identified as folk devils in the study of clashes taking place in the 1960s?

5. What did Schlesinger and Tumber find about individuals who watched a lot of TV and read a lot of newspapers?

6. What is meant by the victim fallacy?

7. What issue do McRobbie and Thornton have with moral panics?

8. Why is cyber-crime difficult to police?

9. What do Cohen and Young state news to be?

10. Roughly what percentage of coverage in newspapers is devoted to crime?

PRACTICE QUESTIONS

Question 1: Outline three ways in which the media misrepresent crime. (6 marks) **Spend 9 minutes on this response.**

> **HINTS TO HELP YOU RESPOND**
> Select three of the fallacies outlined by Marcus Felson. Note each on a separate line with a brief explanation next to each. For example: An age fallacy – the media shows victims and criminals as more likely to be older rather than younger, as suggested in official statistics.

> **Item A**
> Moral panics are often created as a result of exaggerated media portrayals of deviant groups in society. Stanley Cohen explained how mods and rockers became folk devils when the media displayed them negatively after clashes between the groups in the 1960s. This negative attention caused a deviance amplification spiral in which further crime was predicted.
>
> Some sociologists see moral panics as a way of establishing a common view against negative behaviour, others view them as a means of distracting attention away from bigger issues in society.

Question 2: Applying material from Item A, analyse two sociological responses to moral panics. (10 marks) **Spend 15 minutes on this response.**

> **HINTS TO HELP YOU RESPOND**
> You must use Item A in your response. Read it carefully and look for two specific responses that you can analyse. Note that the final paragraph shows both a functionalist and neo-Marxist response to moral panics. You need to explain each in a detailed PEEEL paragraph. For example: Functionalist sociologists may see moral panics as a means of 'establishing a common view against negative behaviour' as suggested in Item A. The moral panic may engage members of society in viewing an act as deviant, allowing them to further affirm actions that are and are not accepted within the norms and values of society. In uniting against a deviant group or action, the collective conscience is strengthened. A newly affirmed awareness of acts viewed as deviant may reduce anomie and ensure that members of society act in a way that provides harmony in society. This view holds moral panics as providing a positive function in society.

Crime and Deviance: Globalisation, Crimes of the State and Green Criminology

Globalisation

Globalisation is the process of interconnectedness of societies across the world. It stems from technological invention, the ease of air travel, and the freedom of businesses to operate across national borders.

As a result of globalisation there has been a change in the quantity and variety of crimes across the world. Manuel Castells (1998) states that the **global criminal economy** is worth over a trillion pounds per annum. Global crime includes: the illegal trafficking of drugs, migrants, arms, tobacco, alcohol, body parts, cultural artefacts and nuclear materials; sex crime, cyber-crime, green crime and terrorism.

Ulrich Beck (1992) notes new insecurities arise from globalisation. Risks are now seen as global rather than local; he calls this **global risk consciousness**. The interconnectedness of countries causes concern about economic migrants and asylum seekers.

EVALUATION POINT

The drugs trade is a prime example of global (transnational) crime. Drugs are trafficked across national borders from developing countries to the western word. The capacity to grow and harvest crops in countries with favourable climates then sell the resulting drugs in wealthier western countries is one result of globalisation.

Deregulation of Businesses

Globalisation has also created increased inequality within society; the wealthy utilise globalisation as a catalyst to create more wealth but those in poverty experience its negative effects. Ian Taylor (1997) observes that large corporations are increasingly able to produce goods in countries with few health and safety regulations and low wages; this leads to frustration over the perceived lack of job opportunities that result from this. A **deregulation** of businesses means that governments lack control over their own economies; this results in a decline in government income, which may be addressed by reducing welfare payments, thus creating further inequality. Deregulation also encourages corporate crimes and poor working terms and conditions, for example zero-hour contracts.

Criminal Organisations

New criminal organisations have been created by globalisation. Hobbs and Dunnigham (1998) examine the rise of **glocal** organisations that have local roots with global links. These are networks rather than criminal hierarchies. The drugs trade is a good example of a glocal organisation with local produce being smuggled to other countries for supply onward.

Misha Glenny (2008) wrote *McMafia*. He examined the impact of the fall of communism on Eastern Europe including Russia. Glenny discovered that with the new Russian government stopping regulation of the economy, prices of food and rent rocketed. Glenny also noted that certain commodities (such as oil and gas) were kept at their old regulated prices; this enabled the wealthy to buy these items cheaply then sell them for substantial profit in other countries. This created a new elite of **oligarchs** who safeguarded their new-found wealth by hiring mafias to protect them.

State Crime

State crimes are illegal or deviant activities committed by the state itself or with the support and/or awareness of the state. Green and Ward (2012) note that state crime "includes all forms of crime committed by, or on behalf of, states and governments in order to further their policies".

The **scale of state crime** and the ability of the state to cover it up or justify its own actions make it a real concern. The **state defines its own laws**, and therefore laws can be passed that allow for actions that cause harm to individuals or the environment. In 1994, **Rwanda** suffered mass genocide enabled by the state. Rwanda was split into Hutus and Tutsis; these two groups were similar and the division was based on perceived social class, with Tutsi ownership of livestock being the main difference in power between the two groups. Hutu members of the government fuelled a race hate campaign against the Tutsis that resulted in more than 800,000 Tutsis being murdered in state-legitimised genocide by the government.

Schwendinger and Schwendinger (1970) believe crime should be defined by acts that violate **human rights** rather than that of breaking a country's laws. States that deny human beings their basic rights should be considered criminal.

Green Crime

Stanley Cohen argues that democratic states have to legitimise their actions. He notes that they use **techniques of neutralisation** to appeal against their criminal or harmful actions.

Green Crime may not break conventional laws. It refers to crimes that cause harm to the environment (including animals). Green criminologists are more radical than traditional criminologists as they focus on **harm** rather than law-breaking; the majority of environmental crimes are not illegal. Green criminology transgresses the boundaries of traditional criminology to include more issues.

Two types of green crime exist. **Primary green crime** is when an act destroys or degrades the Earth's resources. These crimes include: deforestation, air pollution, water pollution, and harm to endangered species. **Secondary green crime** arises from breaking rules that exist to protect the Earth's resources and prevent environmental disaster.

Treatment of the Earth's Resources

There are two views surrounding the treatment of the Earth's resources. The **anthropocentric view** believes human beings have the power and authority to do what they want with the environment, putting financial gain before harm to nature. The **ecocentric view** is used by green criminologists; human beings and nature are interdependent, human beings must respect the planet because they are reliant on it.

- Globalisation has provided new opportunities for crime through a growing interconnectedness of countries and advancements in technology.

- New insecurities, which occur as a result of globalisation, mean there is now a global risk consciousness.

- Large corporations are able to move production to low-wage countries causing job insecurity. Businesses have become deregulated, which means that states have less control of their economies.

- Globalisation has produced new criminal structures such as global organisations and the McMafia.

- State crime is a major issue due to its scale and the ability of states to control their own laws.

- Many sociologists suggest that crime should be defined to include all acts that violate human rights.

- Primary green crime and secondary green crime cause harm to the environment. Green criminologists take an ecocentric view of harm to nature and the planet.

QUICK TEST

1. According to Manuel Castells how much is the global criminal economy worth?

2. What do green criminologists focus on rather than law–breaking?

3. What is primary green crime?

4. What has caused a lack of power held by governments to control their own economies?

5. What view of harm believes that humans have power and authority to use the Earth for their own financial gain?

6. What does Ulrich Beck mean by global risk consciousness?

7. Where did a vast genocide take place with a mainly Hutu government killing many Tutsis?

8. What is a glocal criminal organisation?

9. What does Glenny call the groups that formed after the fall of communist power in Russia and Eastern Europe?

10. Why has globalisation caused job insecurity in many areas of the UK?

PRACTICE QUESTIONS

Item A
Globalisation is the growing interconnectedness of societies, it arises as a result of cheaper air travel, advancements in technology and a range of other factors. The ability to form easy links with others across the globe has resulted in a number of new forms of criminal organisations. Sociologists have suggested that local crimes can now be influenced by global links. The fall of communism created groups such as the Chechen mafia with vast amounts of wealth.

Question 1: Applying material from Item A, analyse two types of criminal organisation that have arisen as a result of globalisation. (10 marks) **Spend 15 minutes on this response.**

HINTS TO HELP YOU RESPOND
You must use points from within Item A. It mentions local crimes with global links, so is clearly asking you to discuss glocal organisations. It also notes the fall of communism, which leads to including the McMafia. Make both of your points detailed PEEL paragraphs. For example: As Item A suggests, the fall of communism led to a rise in crime. Misha Glenny noted that in Russia and Eastern European areas a rise in the McMafia occurred when communism fell. Commodities that had their prices regulated by the state rose in price; however, in some cases (for example, oil) these prices remained low. The few people with wealth were able to buy these commodities in vast quantities at low prices. They were then able to sell these on across national borders to make vast profits. The ease at which transactions can occur across borders is a direct result of globalisation and has facilitated a rise in wealth leading to a need for protection for those with vast amounts of money. Mafia-style organisations were established to protect this wealth.

Question 2: Outline two types of green crime. (4 marks) **Spend 6 minutes on this response.**

HINTS TO HELP YOU RESPOND
Start each point on a new line. Be brief in your responses. For example: Primary green crime consists of crimes that directly result in the destruction and degradation of the Earth's resources.

Secondary green crime results from the flouting of regulations that serve to protect the environment.

Crime and Deviance: Control in Society and Victimisation

Punishment

Punishment in society can be justified for a number of reasons. It can act as a **deterrent** against crime occurring; it can **rehabilitate** offenders and thus prevent further crime; it can **incapacitate** an offender so that they aren't physically able to reoffend; or it can act as **retribution** by taking revenge on the criminal on behalf of society.

Emile Durkheim suggested that punishment serves to reinforce **social solidarity** in society, strengthening the **collective conscience** (value consensus) by expressing the views that some acts will not be tolerated. He notes that the type of justice adopted through punishment reflects the society in which it is used. Traditional societies use **retributive justice**, which tends to be severe and focuses on revenge; the collective conscience is stronger. In modern society **restitutive justice** exists; it focuses more on the relationship between individuals and tries to repair the damage done by the criminal act (for example, through community service).

EVALUATION POINT

Marxists propose that punishment does not strengthen society but creates further **class conflict** between the ruling class and lower classes. The objective of punishment is to defend the property of the ruling class, reflecting their dominant position in society. Prison is the main punishment as it forces the lower classes to give up their time. In a capitalist society time is money and time is all that the lower classes own.

Enforcement of Punishment

In 1977 Michel Foucault wrote *Discipline and Punish* which examines the acts of two different types of power in society and how each enforces punishments. **Sovereign power** is exerted in premodern society.

The body is physically punished, often through torture. **Disciplinary power** is more prevalent in today's society; the body is not punished or controlled but the mind is. Foucault used a prison design called the **panopticon** to illustrate how this control operates in society. In the panopticon there is a central guard tower in which the guards are not visible to the prisoners; cells surround this tower but the prisoners do not know when they are being watched. This causes the prisoners to act as though they are constantly being watched. This enables the control to take place inside the prisoner. Foucault states that this type of surveillance takes place in the majority of institutions in modern society.

EVALUATION POINT

Foucault focuses too much on the extent of control that takes place in individuals, suggesting that there is no ability to resist it. Goffman (1982) notes that some inmates are able to resist such controls, particularly in mental hospitals. Thomas Mathiesen (1997) argues that media advances now mean that rather than those in power watching those without power everyone now watches everyone else in a **synopticon**.

Prison

Before the Industrial Revolution Europe used a variety of types of punishment from flogging to execution; since then prison has become the most severe form of punishment (in comparison to other forms such as ASBOs and curfews). The usefulness of prison is disputed with so many prisoners reoffending. In order to win votes, politicians promise tougher sentences (**popular punitiveness**). This has caused an increase in the prison population in which young males and ethnic minority groups are over-represented. Some individuals end up locked in a cycle of control, being transferred from one institution to the next rather than receiving the help to resolve the situation; this is known as **transcarceration**.

Crime Prevention Measures

Crime prevention measures come in a variety of formats; instead of punishing, they aim to regulate behaviour.

Right realists Wilson and Kelling (1982) use the **broken windows theory** to suggest that signs of disorder in society (from graffiti to littering) should be tackled immediately; this lets individuals know that crime is not accepted in the community (see also the chapter on 'Crime and Deviance: Realism and Crime'). Improving the environment with a display of control helps members of society feel supported in standing up against crime. They believe that this **environmental approach** should be paired with zero-tolerance policing to prevent serious crimes taking root.

Situation crime prevention aims to tackle crime before it has happened. It works on the right realist view that criminals make a **rational choice** when deciding whether or not to commit a crime. **Target hardening** measures change an area to design out crime, thus increasing the difficulty of committing crimes.

Social and Community Crime Prevention

Left realists argue that **social and community crime prevention** is most effective. Instead of zero-tolerance policing, policies should aim to tackle the root cause of crime: poverty. By providing job opportunities and housing, crime will be reduced. The Perry Preschool Project, a longitudinal study that provided an enrichment programme for disadvantaged 3-4 year olds in Michigan, USA, is an example of this in practice. Those who took part in the project were less likely to offend in adult life (compared to those who didn't participate in the project).

Victims of Crime

There are two approaches to the study of **victims** of crime. Nils Christie (1986) argues that the concept of a victim is socially constructed. He states that the media and criminal justice system have a view of the **ideal victim** as weak and blameless, often portraying victims as female or elderly. **Positivist victimology** examines patterns of victimisation to discover the traits of victims that add to their **victim proneness** (the likeliness of falling victim to crime); these traits include low levels of intelligence. Positivist victimologists also examine **victim precipitation** in which victims trigger the events that lead to their own victimisation.

Critical victimologists focus on examining the **structural factors** in society that cause greater risk of victimisation, such as social class or gender. They are concerned with the state's ability to deny an individual the label of victim.

SUMMARY

- Punishment can be used as a deterrent from crime, to rehabilitate, to incapacitate, or as a means of retribution.

- Functionalists suggest punishment aids to reinforce the collective conscience and re-establish social solidarity. Traditional societies use retributive justice. Modern societies use restorative justice.

- Foucault examines the shift from sovereign power to disciplinary power, explaining changes in control in society using the example of the panopticon.

- Prison populations have risen as a result of popular punitiveness. Many groups in society are at risk of transcarceration.

- Right realist crime prevention measures involve an environmental approach that uses broken windows theory. They also use target hardening and zero-tolerance policing as situational crime prevention measures.

- Left realists prefer social and community crime prevention measures such as the Perry Preschool Project, which aim to tackle the root causes of crime.

- The media and criminal justice system have a set view of the ideal victim.

- Positivist victimology examines victim proneness and victim precipitation.

- Critical victimology focuses on the structural factors in society that cause crime.

QUICK TEST

1. Which type of justified punishment looks at physically preventing a criminal from reoffending (committing another crime)?

2. What is the name of the prison used in Foucault's example of power?

3. What term do positivist victimologists use for traits that cause a person to be more likely to fall victim to crime?

4. According to Foucault what type of power is used in modern societies?

5. What term describes a government's promise to clamp down on certain crimes in order to win votes?

6. What theory suggests that signs of vandalism and graffiti should be tackled immediately before serious crimes take root?

7. What type of crime prevention do left realists prefer?

8. What type of justice aims to repair situations by fixing the damage that they have caused?

9. Which term describes that movement of an individual from one agency of social control to another?

10. What is meant by target hardening?

PRACTICE QUESTIONS

Item A
Ron Clarke (1992) is a right realist who favours a pre-emptive approach to crime prevention, adopting a situational crime prevention that aims to reduce opportunities for crime. This approach to crime prevention is favoured by sociologists who believe crime to be the result of a choice, evaluating strengths and weaknesses of the criminal act.

Other sociologists disagree and see crime prevention as only having real effect when the structural causes within society that create crime are reduced. These sociologists favour prevention methods that reduce inequality in society.

Question 1: Applying material from Item A and your own knowledge, evaluate the right realist view of crime prevention. (30 marks) **Spend 45 minutes on this response.**

HINTS TO HELP YOU RESPOND
Explain the causes of crime according to right realists and link these to Item A, noting Ron Clarke's stance on situational crime prevention. Explain target hardening and then critique this with displacement, giving examples if possible. Continue to explain the right realist view of broken windows theory and evaluate this with its lack of identifying the structural causes of crime. In your evaluation use left realism and the Perry Preschool Project as an explanation of the importance of tackling structural causes of crime; your response could also link to Marxism. Continue to evaluate this with the right realist theory that crime is an active choice and that poverty is not a direct cause of crime. Ensure that you make strong links back to the question in each point made.

Question 2: Outline two reasons why punishment is justified. (4 marks) **Spend 6 minutes on this response.**

HINTS TO HELP YOU RESPOND
You can select from any of the four reasons mentioned within the chapter: rehabilitation, as a deterrent, to incapacitate, or as retribution. Start each one on a new line and add a quick sentence explaining the two that you use. For example: Rehabilitation – punishment may serve to change the lives of offenders through impacting on them in order to ensure that they do not reoffend.

Sociological Theory: Quantitative and Qualitative Methodology

Quantitative research methods gather numerical data that can be used to find correlations; these include: questionnaires, structured interviews and official statistics. **Qualitative** research methods give insight into the meanings behind the actions and lives of the study participants; these include: unstructured interviews, participant observation and personal documents.

Methodology

Sociologists' use of methodology is impacted upon by **practical issues**. These include: **time and costs**, the **personal skills** of the researcher, the restrictions of the **subject matter** being researched, the requirements put in place by **funding bodies**, and the **opportunities** available to the researcher. (For more information about these see *Letts A-Level Sociology In A Week Book 1*.)

When conducting research **ethical issues** must also be taken into account. There are a number of aspects that sociologists must consider. They must ensure that **informed consent** is given and collected; they must keep participants' details **private and confidential**; they must take care when studying **vulnerable groups**; they must aim to reduce harmful **physical and psychological effects** on participants; and they must take care when conducting **covert** research to avoid deception.

Theoretical issues impact on a study's reliability, its ability to gather the same results if repeated. Quantitative methods are more **reliable** because they often follow a **standardised procedure**. Research aims to gather **validity**, the true picture of the events or concepts it is studying. Qualitative methods are more likely to be valid due to their in-depth approach and ability to achieve **empathy**. Research aims to be **representative** by taking a typical cross-section of society as a sample; larger samples tend to be more representative.

EVALUATION POINT

It is difficult to ensure that sociological research reaches a balance between validity, reliability and representativeness. Different theoretical approaches place the emphasis on achieving a balance between the three concepts that reflect their priorities.

Positivists

Positivists prefer the use of quantitative methods because they believe that sociology should be modelled on the natural sciences, that society can be studied objectively. Sociologists must be able to avoid impacting emotionally on research so as to produce objective **social facts** about society. Positivists believe that individuals in society are shaped by the social patterns that exist. Social patterns can be displayed through trends found within research, such as police statistics displaying minority ethnic groups being more likely to face arrest, or exam results showing that those from low-income households are more likely to underachieve.

EVALUATION POINT

Interpretivists argue that quantitative methods are not relevant to the study of human beings. The view that individuals are shaped by forces in society neglects to acknowledge free will. Interpretivists propose a subjective approach to the study of society is relevant.

Positivists' Research Methods

Positivists favour the following research methods:

- **Laboratory experiments** take place in a controlled environment and follow a standardised procedure, making them reliable. They measure differences in results between a **control group** and an **experimental group** in order to establish cause and effect relationships.

EVALUATION POINT

It is difficult to study humans in the artificial environment of a laboratory as it is a closed system and the world around an individual is an open system where more variables impact on each situation than do within a laboratory. Only small samples can be studied due to space constrictions. Participants may experience the Hawthorne effect or expectancy effect causing the method to lack validity. Field experiments aim to reduce some of these constrictions as they take place in the natural environment.

- **Questionnaires** consist of pre-set questions that require either **closed-ended** or **open-ended** responses. Most questionnaires use closed-ended (or fixed) responses so that the answers are easy to categorise and quantify. They are cheap and quick to distribute and can reach large samples, making them representative.

EVALUATION POINT

Questionnaires may have a low **response rate**, or simply only responses from those who have time to take part, thus impacting on their representativeness. It is also easy to lie on a questionnaire, casting doubts over validity.

- **Structured interviews** have fixed questions like a questionnaire. They can be conducted either face-to-face or by telephone. Due to the set questions they are reasonably quick to conduct, and answers can be quantified as they often contain closed-ended responses.

EVALUATION POINT

Questions are inflexible meaning that the researcher is not able to pursue areas of interest or guide the research to gather depth; this impacts on validity.

- **Official statistics** are produced by the government and other official bodies. They include the rate of births, deaths and marriages, school exam results, police records and the census. They are sometimes compulsory and gathered as a legal requirement, which means that they are naturally representative.

EVALUATION POINT

Some official statistics can be considered to be **soft statistics** as they can be debated; for example, police records only show crimes recorded by the police, omitting actions that are reported but not recorded. These omitted statistics are known as the **dark figure of crime**.

Interpretivists' Research Methods

Interpretivists favour the following research methods:

- **Unstructured interviews** are more like a flexible conversation and allow the researcher to pursue their own line of questioning, to clarify answers and ask follow-up questions if necessary. They enable the researcher to develop a rapport with the interviewee, encouraging more truthful responses, ensuring that the findings are valid.

EVALUATION POINT

Unstructured interviews are time-consuming and require a trained interviewer. They also provide open responses that are hard to quantify in order to analyse findings. Only small samples are likely to be used, making them lack representativeness.

● **Participant observation** allows the researcher to gain **insight** into the lives and actions of those they are observing. **Covert** observation allows for the researcher to see real life behaviour at first hand.

EVALUATION POINT

Getting access to groups to observe them can often be difficult, especially if the research is covert. The researcher will not be able to gather informed consent, which causes ethical implications for the research. Participant observation is time-consuming and it may be difficult for the researcher to make notes while observing.

● **Personal documents** such as diaries, letters and emails allow sociologists to study past events and these may include notes about the writer's personal feelings and motives. These can be highly valid.

QUICK TEST

1. What type of data do positivists prefer?

2. Why might covert observation cause ethical implications for the researcher?

3. What do positivists believe individuals to be shaped by in society?

4. What is meant by a research method being reliable?

5. Who are official statistics gathered by?

6. What are soft statistics?

7. What type of responses do most questionnaires gather?

8. What two groups are the sample spilt into in experiments?

9. Why might laboratory experiments lack validity?

10. What makes quantitative methods more reliable?

SUMMARY

● **Quantitative research methods gather numerical data that can be used to find correlations and cause-and-effect relationships.**

● **Qualitative research methods give insight into the meanings that individuals attach to their actions.**

● **Practical, ethical and theoretical issues must be taken into account by the sociologist when deciding upon which research method to use.**

● **Positivists prefer quantitative methods as their main goals are reliability and representativeness. They like to find cause-and-effect relationships in order to discover social facts.**

● **Positivists favour laboratory experiments, questionnaires, structured interviews and official statistics.**

● **Interpretivists prefer qualitative methods as their main goal is that of validity.**

● **Interpretivists favour unstructured interviews, participant observation and personal documents.**

PRACTICE QUESTIONS

Item A

Positivists aim to gather representative findings that are able to show cause-and-effect relationships in order to discover social facts. They believe individuals in society to be shaped by the social patterns around them. They prefer methods that allow the researcher to act objectively and detach themselves from the research process as much as possible. Positivists believe that sociology should reflect the natural sciences in its methodology.

In comparison, other sociologists see quantitative methods as ineffective ways of studying individuals.

Question 1: Applying material from Item A and your own knowledge, evaluate the positivist approach to methodology. (20 marks) **Spend 30 minutes on this response.**

HINTS TO HELP YOU RESPOND

Start by using the item to explain the basic positivist view of methodology. Note the main goal of representativeness, explain what this is, and also the goal of reliability. State that positivists favour an objective, scientific approach to the study of society. Evaluate these by mentioning the interpretivist argument that human beings are too complex to be studied using methods that fail to gather insight and depth, explain the view that qualitative methods are better when aiming for validity. Use different examples of methods and their strengths and weaknesses to support your arguments. Make sure you link each point to the question.

Question 2: Outline and explain two practical problems faced within sociological research. (10 marks) **Spend 15 minutes on this response.**

HINTS TO HELP YOU RESPOND

Two detailed PEEEL paragraphs are needed here. Make sure you separate your points clearly. You can focus on any of the practical issues mentioned within the chapter, from funding body requirements through to the time-consuming nature of some methods. For example: Sociologists must take into account the practical constraints of the time that they have available to them when deciding upon which method to use. Interpretivist sociologists will require more time to conduct their research as they aim to gather qualitative data. Most qualitative methods are lengthy in order to ensure that true insight can be gained to gather valid findings. For example, participant observation means that the researcher will have to spend time gaining access to the group they are observing even before the research starts. Quantitative methods may be less time-consuming as the findings are easy to analyse.

Sociological Theory: Marxism

Karl Marx (1818-1883) believed that it was possible to study society scientifically. Marxism is a part of the **Enlightenment Project**, a belief that knowledge discovered about society through scientific means could be used to create a better world. Marx's ideas became the basis of **communism** used by the Soviet Union.

Communism

As a conflict theorist, Marx held a number of beliefs about society. Historically, human beings' **material needs** (such as shelter, food and water) were met by humans themselves, working unaided without tools. Over time people began to develop tools and co-operate with others and share the labour in meeting material needs, developing **social relations of production**. As production became more advanced the social relations of production changed. This eventually led to a division between two social classes: a class who owns the **means of production**, **the bourgeoisie** or ruling class, and a class who own nothing but their ability to labour, the **proletariat**, or wage-slaves.

Once human history had developed past its earliest stage (**primitive communism**, where there were no class divisions because everything was shared) a different type of society with differing class systems emerged. Marx believed there to have once been three class societies:

1. **Ancient society** – with a class of slaves and a class of landowners who **exploited** them.
2. **Feudal society** – where serfs were tied to an area of land which they had to legally work.
3. **Capitalist society** – where wage-slaves were forced to work for the ruling class.

Each of the three societies is based on the exploitation of one class by another.

EVALUATION POINT

Max Weber suggests that Marx's view of a two-class system is too simplistic. He argues that within these classes there are further divisions.

Capitalism

Marx believed **capitalism** to be based on the division between the bourgeoisie and proletariat. The proletariat are not legally bound to work for the bourgeoisie but they must however sell their labour in exchange for wages to meet their material needs. Marx notes that **competition** causes there to be fewer and fewer owners of the means of production. Small businesses fail to be able to compete with the massive wealth of transnational corporations. Capitalism encourages the pursuit of wealth. Technological advancements mean that machines can do the work of many labourers, **de-skilling** the workforce and causing further **class polarisation**. Capitalism causes the divide between a minority capitalist class (bourgeoisie) and the working class (proletariat).

EVALUATION POINT

The ten largest multinational corporations own almost everything that people can purchase in a supermarket. This supports Marx's view that competition causes fewer people to own more.

Revolution

Class polarisation can create a '**class consciousness**' within the working class when they realise they are being exploited. The proletariat become aware of the need to **overthrow** capitalism.

The ruling class who own the means of production also own the **mental production** in society. They are dominant and therefore their ideas have a dominant position in the ruling of society from within religion and the education system and throughout the media. The proletariat become aware of this when they struggle in society and their class consciousness develops. There is a loss of control over the labour and products that the proletariat make for the bourgeoisie. They become **alienated** as capitalism causes them to become separated from the forces of production, further intensifying the **division of labour**.

Marx predicted that a **proletarian revolution** will occur overthrowing capitalism, abolishing the class system and creating a communist classless society.

> ## EVALUATION POINT
>
> Marx's view that a revolution will occur in society with the proletariat overthrowing capitalism is difficult to disprove. Marxism is hard to fault as Marxists could argue that the revolution is still due to happen. Marx fails to recognise that human beings have free will and can choose how to respond to their position in society.

Humanistic Marxism

Two more modern adaptations of Marxism have developed, partly as a result of the lack of revolution in society. **Humanistic Marxism**, supported by Gramsci, combines aspects of social action theories and **Structuralist Marxism**, supported by Althusser, adopts aspects of positivism.

Gramsci examines the concept of '**hegemony**', the ruling-class ownership and control of ideas and values. He identifies this as key to the ruling class maintaining their dominant position in society. Gramsci notes that **coercion** by the police, army, law courts and other agencies of social control forces the working class to accept ruling-class rules. He also argues that hegemony provides a platform for the ruling class to persuade the working class that their rules are legitimate, making the proletariat accept these rules as fair.

In addition, Gramsci notes that the ruling class do not have complete control as they are still obliged to make deals with other classes, due to their minority in numbers. He suggests that the proletariat experience of poverty and exploitation causes them to develop a **dual consciousness** through which they are aware of the dominant ideology. Gramsci focuses less on the economy; unlike Marx, he believes that a change in **ideas** is central for revolution, rather than **economic determinism**.

> ## EVALUATION POINT
>
> Gramsci overplays the notion of ideas being a key catalyst for revolution. He fails to acknowledge the influence of financial constraints and fear of reprisals from the ruling class as major influences that prevent revolution.

Structuralist Marxism

Althusser is a structuralist Marxist who believes history to be shaped by the structures of society, rather than by the individuals within it. Althusser rejects Marx's ideas of economic determinism and also Garmsci's humanistic view. Althusser's structural determinism sees capitalist society as having three levels: an **economic level**, a **political level**, and an **ideological level**. He sees the economic level as the crux of capitalist society, although he believes the other levels are indispensable. He observes the state using two sets of apparatus to ensure that capitalism continues: the **repressive state apparatus** (RSA) uses physical force to coerce the working class to comply (the army and the police); the **ideological state apparatus** (ISA) uses a network of thoughts and ideas in order to manipulate the working class into accepting capitalism as a legitimate system.

Althusser believes that socialism will only come about as the result of a change in consciousness. He suggests that the three levels of capitalist society function independently of each other.

> ## EVALUATION POINT
>
> Althusser has been criticised for failing to acknowledge the struggle that working-class individuals face in society, and how this can change society. Althusser fails to see the importance of human action and consciousness by only looking at society from a macroscopic perspective.

SUMMARY

- Marxism is a part of the Enlightenment Project. It sees the structure of society as based around material needs.

- A class society formed due to the ownership of the means of production of the bourgeoisie and the proletariat owning nothing but their own labour.

- Marx suggests that there have been three class societies, all based on exploitation: ancient society, feudal society and capitalist society.

- Capitalist society is based on class division with the proletariat becoming de-skilled, resulting in class polarisation and alienation.

- Marx predicted a proletariat revolution.

- Gramsci's humanist Marxism focuses on the concept of hegemony and the ability of the ruling class to coerce the working class into accepting their rules.

- Althusser's structuralist view identifies three structural levels in society: an economic level, a political level and an ideological level.

- He notes the use of the RSA and ISA in ensuring that capitalism continues in society.

QUICK TEST

1. What is meant by the Enlightenment Project?

2. According to Marx, what type of society had slaves and landowners who exploited them?

3. What is meant by the term hegemony?

4. What term is given to the awareness of the working class that they are being exploited due to their position in society?

5. What did Marx believe would happen in order to overthrow capitalism?

6. What is an ideological state apparatus?

7. Which term is used for the ruling, or capitalist, class?

8. What causes there to be fewer and fewer owners of the means of production?

9. According to Gramsci, what does the proletariat experience of poverty and exploitation cause them to develop?

10. What are the three levels of the capitalist society according to Althusser?

PRACTICE QUESTIONS

Question 1: Outline and explain two key concepts of Marxism. (10 marks) **Spend 15 minutes on this response.**

HINTS TO HELP YOU RESPOND

Select any two key concepts from the de-skilling of the workforce through to a proletariat revolution. Explain each in its own detailed PEEEL paragraph. For example: Marx sees society as based on a class division with the proletariat becoming increasingly de-skilled. The bourgeoisie own the means of production and require the proletariat to work as wage-slaves in order to support their wealth. With technological advancements the proletariat are not needed for as many of the skilled positions as previously. This de-skills the proletariat causing a further class divide between them and the bourgeoisie and further alienating them from the production of goods.

Item A

Traditional Marxists see society as based on a class division between the proletariat and bourgeoisie. They suggest that exploitation due to one group owning the means of production over the other exists in society. Marxists note that a classless society will exist as a result of a proletariat revolution.

Other sociologists argue that a class division between two groups in society is no longer evident, they also voice concerns that a proletariat revolution is yet to happen.

Question 2: Applying material from Item A and your own knowledge, evaluate the usefulness of Marxist explanations of society. (20 marks) **Spend 30 minutes on this response.**

HINTS TO HELP YOU RESPOND

Explain traditional Marxist views about the structure of society using Item A, mentioning Marxism as a conflict perspective. Note the aims of society to meet material needs and the progression from this to a class society. Explain class consciousness and alienation of the working class. Support these with examples of inequality in education, the family, and crime and deviance. Explain Gramsci's humanist Marxism, evaluate this using Althusser's structural view of Marxism. You can use concepts from functionalism to argue against the class divide.

Sociological Theory: Functionalism

Functionalism is a consensus approach that has its origins in the works of Emile Durkheim who believed society to exist separately from its individual members, shaping their behaviour. Durkheim noted the differences between a traditional society and a modern, more complex, society. He suggests that in **traditional society** the majority of people were similar, a good **collective conscience** existed, and there were strongs bonds of attachment between individuals and society. There was no real individuality, people regarded themselves as part of the society around them.

The Collective Conscience

In **modern society** there has become a **complex division of labour**. This division causes groups to fulfil different roles and weakens the **collective conscience**. Durkheim believed that for society to work effectively individuals must be prevented from developing **egoistic** (selfish) attitudes, and they must be **regulated** in order to accomplish this. He saw swift change in society as a negative: it causes **anomie**, a sense of normlessness, weakening **social cohesion**.

EVALUATION POINT

Marxists would suggest that the collective conscience in society is that of the dominant, capitalist class. This causes a natural division in society as class consciousness develops and the proletariat disconnect from the collective ideas due to a growing awareness of their exploitation.

Parsons' Organic Analogy

Talcott Parsons says society is similar to the human body. He outlines three links between the body and society in his organic analogy:

1. **system** – society and the body each regulate themselves. They are made up of interconnected parts that fit together to serve each other.

2. **system needs** – just as the body has physical needs that must be met to survive, so too does society. Socialisation into the shared norms and values of society is a need that must be met.

3. **functions** – each part of society must perform a function for the smooth running of society as a whole, just like organs in the body.

EVALUATION POINT

You can support Parsons' organic analogy with aspects of the family, education, media and even crime. Each of these performs functions for society. For example, crime acts to reaffirm the boundaries of society.

The Value Consensus

Parsons believes that social order is only possible if individuals have a shared culture, or common interest in a central set of norms and values. He calls this shared set of norms and values the **value consensus**. Individuals must be effectively **integrated** into society to ensure this value consensus exists. Parsons notes two functions of society that ensure the value consensus exists. Firstly, **social control** must exist through which negative and positive behaviour are effectively sanctioned. Secondly, **socialisation** must be conducted by the family and education system to ensure that individuals are instilled with the collective values of society.

The structural system of society is analogised by Parsons as a building consisting of different vital parts. The base of society is **norms**, which guide individuals' behaviour; next are **status-roles**, which are specific norms particular to each person's role in society, instructing them (and others) how they should act. Next, there are **institutions** consisting of individuals with a variety of different status-roles; for example, the family or education system. Beyond this are **subsystems** made up of interdependent institutions. Over all these parts is the **social system** (society as a whole).

Parsons sees individuals as direct products of the society around them. His view that individuals will conform to the value consensus as a result of effective socialisation and social control can be regarded as too deterministic. Interpretivists argue that an individual's free will can determine their own actions instead of them being a puppet of society.

Parsons' AGIL Schema

Parson's **AGIL schema** outlines the four requirements of society:

1. **Adaptation** – society must adapt to meet an individual's material needs.
2. **Goal attainment** – society must set goals for people to strive for and also provide the necessary resources for them to do so.
3. **Integration** – subsystems must integrate with each other to work towards the shared goals of society.
4. **Latency** – processes must exist that allow society to continue to function. These can include functions that ensure individuals can manage stress.

Parsons notes that in traditional societies status is **ascribed**, people are treated with **pluralistic standards**, and the group is more important than individuals. In modern society people **achieve a** status, they are more focused on themselves, and the same set of rules applies to everyone. Parsons believes that social change occurs gradually as society becomes more complex; institutions within the subsystem develop with specialist functions to meet society's needs. He calls this process **structural differentiation**.

Robert Merton believed Parsons was wrong in assuming that society always runs smoothly and successfully integrates individuals into accepting shared norms and values. He suggests Parsons is naive in assuming indispensability, that every part of society is needed: sometimes **functional alternatives** may fulfil a similar function, only differently. Parsons also assumes **functional unity**, that all parts work for the whole structure. Merton argues that some functions work independently and have functional autonomy from others. Merton also notices that Parsons assumes that all functions are positive, that some functions may serve some groups and not others; he calls this assumption **universal functionalism**.

Manifest and Latent Functions

Merton is, however, a key functionalist. He sees two types of function in society. **Manifest functions** are intended and actively aim to do good for society. **Latent functions** are unintended; for example, the impact of a disaster in society may reinforce social solidarity as individuals support each other.

It could be argued that functionalism is not scientific as its claims cannot be falsified. Marxists also dispute the usefulness of functionalism as they see it as a conservative viewpoint that serves to legitimise the unequal structure of society.

SUMMARY

- Durkheim noted the movement from traditional to modern society where a more complex division of labour needed individuals to be regulated to prevent anomie and egoism.

- Parsons saw society like a body. The organic analogy sees three comparisons between the body and society: system, system needs and functions.

- Parsons states a value consensus exists across society. It exists due to effective socialisation and social control.

- Society is organised like a building according to Parsons with norms, status-roles, institutions and subsystems making up the social system.

- The needs of society are explained in Parsons' AGIL schema. These are adaptation, goal attainment, integration and latency.

- Merton applies a functionalist criticism to Parsons, stating that there are functional alternatives in society and that Parsons' views of functional unity and universal functionalism are flawed.

- Merton suggests that there are manifest functions and latent functions in society.

QUICK TEST

1. What does Parsons call the shared norms and values of society?

2. What are the four functions in Parsons' AGIL schema?

3. What does Merton suggest is available, meaning that some institutions in society are not indispensable?

4. Which term describes the similarities between the human body and society?

5. What two types of functions exist in society according to Merton?

6. Which term describes the selfishness that Durkheim suggests needs to be avoided in society?

7. What is meant by the term anomie?

8. What do subsystems consist of in Parson's explanation of society?

9. Why can it be argued that functionalism is not scientific?

10. What does Parsons mean by the term status-roles?

PRACTICE QUESTIONS

Question 1: Outline and explain two of society's needs according to Parsons. (10 marks) **Spend 15 minutes on this response.**

> **HINTS TO HELP YOU RESPOND**
> Select any two parts of the AGIL schema to use. Make your points in two detailed PEEEL paragraphs. For example: According to Parsons, society should provide goal attainment. It should encourage individuals and institutions to work towards the completion of goals that serve themselves and society as a whole. In order for this to work society must also provide the structure and resources needed for individuals to effectively achieve their goals. The goal of the education system may be to prepare children for the world of work; teachers and students must be provided with the resources needed to ensure that they can work towards this goal which will, in turn, benefit society.

> **Item A**
> Functionalism is based around the works of Emile Durkheim who saw society as being able to benefit from the findings of scientific study. Durkheim noted the movement from traditional society to modern society causing changes to the division of labour. Functionalists believe that society is made up of interdependent parts, which operate for the smooth running of society as a whole, with individuals sharing a collective conscience of shared norms and values.
>
> Other sociologists claim that the functionalist view of society fails to note inequality between social groups and may also neglect to note the power of the individual and their free will.

Question 2: Applying material from Item A and your own knowledge, evaluate the usefulness of the functionalist explanation of society. (20 marks) **Spend around 30 minutes on this response.**

> **HINTS TO HELP YOU RESPOND**
> Use Item A to explain the basic views of Durkheim. Explain the complex division of labour and the need to avoid a weakening of collective conscience. Support Durkheim by explaining Parsons' organic analogy. Continue to explain the structure of society according to Parsons and his AGIL schema. Use Merton to critique Parsons, explaining functional alternatives. You can also apply evaluation from Marxism, feminist or action theories focusing on the fundamental differences between conflict and consensus views.

Sociological Theory: Feminism

Feminists are concerned with a **patriarchal** (male-led) society and the **subordination** of women within this system. Feminism's impact on politics began with the **suffragette** campaign for the women's vote in the 19th century. From a sociological perspective feminism is a conflict approach and also a **political movement**.

Radical Feminists

Radical feminists focus heavily on the concept of patriarchy. It is rooted in changes in society in the 1960s when women led antiwar rallies and New Left political movements. Shulamith Firestone (1974) notes that **patriarchy is universal** due to a woman's ability to give birth and care for children, because of this women are forced to become dependent on men. Radical feminism sees patriarchy as the **main form of inequality** in society and they believe **all men oppress women**. They state that all men benefit from the inequality in society as a result of women's unpaid labour in the domestic role. Radical feminists see patriarchy as ruling everywhere in society from the home to the workplace and as a result they believe it to be **personal**.

Radical feminists observe that all relationships in society involve power, and that this makes them **political relationships**; this also includes relationships within the family. The fear of women who are afraid to go out at night stems from the potential threat of physical male violence and is an example of patriarchal power in society. **Malestream sociology** views sexuality as a biological urge and therefore outside the scope of sociology. Radical feminists disagree and argue that patriarchy is a **social construct**.

Relationships in society must change to enable **women's liberation**. Some radical feminists believe that living separately from men in a form of **separatism** could lead to freedom and independence. **Raising consciousness** among women to highlight their oppression may lead to collective responses to inequality. A few radical feminists believe that **political lesbianism** may be the key to changing society and fighting against the oppression faced in heterosexual relationships.

Marxist Feminists

Marxist feminists argue that **capitalism** creates the subordination of women in order to benefit its cause. The subordination of women serves a number of functions in society. Firstly, women **reproduce the labour force** as they offer unpaid labour to support the male workers. Secondly, women act as a **reserve army of labour** that can be employed to suit the needs of capitalism, treated as though their main role is in the home and that any paid work is a bonus for them. Thirdly, women act as a **vent for the aggression** and frustration of male workers who have been exploited in the workplace.

In order to change the oppression of women, Marxist sociologist Michele Barrett suggests that we should look at the **ideology of the family**. The **nuclear family** is presented as ideal and normal, its structure promotes a sexual division of labour; it is also shown as the only place where a woman can be fulfilled. Barrett suggests that in order to overthrow capitalism this ideology of the family must be changed. Eve Mitchell notes that the **unconscious ideas of femininity** are so deeply rooted in women and society that they will be difficult to change.

Dual Systems Feminists

Dual systems feminists combine the concepts of Marxist and radical feminism. Hartmann notes that capitalism and patriarchy are interconnected, calling this **patriarchal capitalism**. Dual systems feminists believe that women's oppression can only be understood by examining their position in both patriarchal and capitalist society. Sylvia Walby argues that these two systems are in conflict as capitalism wants women to be a cheap, exploitable workforce but patriarchy wants women in the domestic role within the family unit.

Liberal Feminists

Liberal or reformist feminists believe that an equality between genders can be achieved in society, and a **gradual reform** can take place through the promotion **of equal rights**. They call for equal pay and equality in the workplace. Liberal feminists see that a **cultural change** is needed to eradicate prejudice and stereotypes that prejudice women, such as the idea that women are controlled by their emotions and thus unable to make rational decisions. These views confine women to the domestic role.

Liberal feminists highlight the need to distinguish between **sex** and **gender**. Sex refers to the physical differences between men and women and gender is a **social construct** defined by different cultural views of masculinity and femininity. They note that sex is a fixed concept and gender has the capacity to change across cultures and time. To change the stereotypical view of gender, the process of **socialisation** must change. Stereotypes shown in the media and educational textbooks are among aspects of socialisation that must change. Men and women are equally capable in society.

Intersectional Feminists

Intersectional feminists see women as a diverse group with many differences that impact on their experiences within a patriarchal society. These include social class, sexual preferences and ethnicity. They criticise other views of feminism as being **essentialist** by suggesting that all women are the same.

Poststructural Feminists

Poststructural feminists are concerned about how people view things in society. They see society as having many different **discourses** (ways of seeing things). They see some discourse as defining acts and individuals in a way that creates inequality. Butler states that the feminist movement is spearheaded by White, middle-class women who misrepresent **universal womanhood**.

SUMMARY

- Feminists are concerned with the subordination of women and inequality in patriarchal society.

- Radical feminists see patriarchy as universal and as the main form of inequality in society. They see every relationship between genders as political.

- Radical feminists see patriarchy as a social construct. They suggest separatism, raising consciousness and political lesbianism as solutions.

- Marxist feminists see capitalism as the source of subordination of women. They see that women reproduce the labour force and act as a reserve army of labour who act as a vent for aggression and frustration.

- Marxist feminists see the ideology of the family and unconscious ideas of femininity as key to creating inequality.

- Dual systems feminists combine the views of radical and Marxist feminists in seeing inequality as caused by patriarchal capitalism.

- Liberal or reformist feminists believe that gradual reform through the promotion of equal rights can occur in society.

- Liberal feminists see gender as a social construct and as a result able to be viewed differently with changes in socialisation.

- Intersectional feminists see other views as essentialist for assuming that all women have the same experience of patriarchal society.

- Poststructural feminists are concerned with discourse in society that causes inequality.

QUICK TEST

1. What is meant by the term patriarchy?

2. According to radical feminists, what makes each relationship in society a political relationship?

3. What do intersectional feminists mean when suggesting that other feminist theories are essentialist?

4. Which type of feminist believes society to be based on patriarchal capitalism?

5. What are discourses?

6. What is the difference between sex and gender for liberal or reformist feminists?

7. Which type of feminist views women as acting as a reserve army of cheap exploitable labour?

8. Which sociologist suggests that capitalism and patriarchy have a conflict of interests?

9. What did Eve Mitchell note as being difficult to change?

10. According to liberal feminists, what needs to be promoted in order to start gradual change in society?

PRACTICE QUESTIONS

Item A
Feminism sees society as patriarchal. Some feminists view this as a deeply ingrained inequality that will only be changed through a separation of the genders. Other feminists see society as gradually changing with equal opportunities being more prevalent in the workplace. Marxist feminists see the combination of two unequal structures across society as the real concern, with class inequality reinforcing patriarchy. Some feminists see capitalism and patriarchy as having a conflict of interest and, in turn, causing issues for each other.

Question 1: Applying material from Item A and your own knowledge, evaluate the usefulness of feminist explanations of society. (20 marks) **Spend 30 minutes on this response.**

HINTS TO HELP YOU RESPOND
Start by explaining the basis of feminism as a conflict approach, link this to the item by discussing patriarchy. Continue to explain the different views of feminist groups using one to evaluate another. For example, use Marxist feminism to discuss the influence of capitalism on patriarchy and note the need for this to be overthrown. Evaluate this with liberal feminism that sees a gradual process as the answer to inequality. You could use dual systems feminism as a support of Marxist feminism and a link to discuss radical feminism. Make sure there are links back to the question with each paragraph.

Question 2: Outline and explain two views of radical feminism. (10 marks) **Spend 15 minutes on this response.**

HINTS TO HELP YOU RESPOND
Use two PEEEL paragraphs to explain any two views of radical feminists from patriarchy being universal to all men oppressing women. For example: Radical feminists see gender inequality as the main form of inequality in society. They view the subordination of women in patriarchal society as key to society's structure. Radical feminists see women as exploited, a cheap expendable form of labour in the domestic role, which is reinforced by society benefiting all men and causing further inequality between men and women in society.

Sociological Theory: Social Action Theories

Action theories are a **micro-level** approach to society, they look at how the actions of individuals in society shape society as a whole. They focus on the power of the individual in society and the **free will** that people are able to assert. Action theories are **voluntaristic** as they see actions as a choice, they favour qualitative methodologies.

> ## EVALUATION POINT
>
> Functionalism and Marxism are structural theories that take a macro-approach to the study of society, they argue that structures in society shape the behaviour of the individuals within them, taking a more deterministic view of behaviour.

The Actions of Individuals

Max Weber suggested that in order to effectively study society, the **structures** in society and **actions** of individuals must both be taken into account. He believed that sociologists should look to explain **the level of cause**, the aims of structural factors in society that shape human behaviour, and also examine **the level of meaning** that each individual attaches to their actions.

From the vast number of meanings that individuals can attach to their actions, Weber came up with four categories:

1. **Traditional action** – actions that are routine in a society or culture, things that have always been done and require no explanation for the individual.
2. **Affective action** – actions that show emotion, such as crying at a sad film.
3. **Rational value-oriented action** – actions influenced by a belief or ideal, for example, a person's religion prompting them to pray.
4. **Rational goal-oriented action** – actions aimed at achieving a goal, with specified benefits for the individual.

> ## EVALUATION POINT
>
> Weber focuses too heavily on the independent views of individuals, he fails to look at shared responses to society.

Symbolic Interactionism

Symbolic interactionism looks at how individuals shape the world around them with their actions. GH Mead explains how individuals use their minds to understand others and decide their own actions. Humans differ from animals because they respond to situations using **rational** thought rather than acting **instinctively**. For instance, if a dog is kicked it will react instinctively; if a human is kicked then they will interpret the situation before reacting.

Blumer outlines three assumptions of symbolic interactionism:

- Individuals have **meanings** for different objects and actions, this influences their response towards them. For example, an image of a heart shows love.
- The meanings people have are based on **social interaction**. For example, if a doctor talks about a heart they won't be talking about love.
- People try and make sense of scenarios adapting their meanings by **reflecting** on situations.

> ## EVALUATION POINT
>
> Marxists and functionalists disagree with Blumer's assumptions as he fails to see how the influence of structures in society (such as poverty) impact on an individual's actions and their interpretation of the world around them.

The Dramaturgical Model

Goffman's **dramaturgical model** sees individuals shaping the way they are treated by others through their own actions. He likens life to a play with individuals as the actors deciding how they present themselves to others. Goffman notes how **impression management** takes place when people decide how they will use the props around them, such as what clothes to wear, or places they will go. He believes people's real selves differ from the **roles** they play in society **on stage** with preparation for these taking place **backstage**.

Labelling Theory

Labelling theory looks at how people **define situations** as real. When a situation is defined as real it has a real consequence. For example, when a person suspects someone of having an affair, they look for actions that support their suspicions (for example, staying late at work); the situation is then seen as real and consequences result from this (for example a confrontation when the person returns). Key labelling theorist Cooley notes that our concept of the **self** comes from how we see the impact of our actions on those around us. Cooley observes that we become what we are seen as.

> ### EVALUATION POINT
>
> Points from education and crime can be used to support the ideas of labelling theorists, such as the self-fulfilling prophecy that results from a teacher's labelling of a pupil impacting on their educational achievements.

Ethnomethodology

Ethnomethodology takes more of a micro-perspective than symbolic interactionism. It studies how individual interactions make order in society possible. Garfinkel notes how individuals work together to create **meanings** and help situations make sense, developing **common sense knowledge**. Not all meanings and situations are understood instantly and individuals must work together to make sense of them: Garfinkel calls this **indexicality**. When individuals use their common sense knowledge to make sense of meanings they are using **reflexivity**. Garfinkel used **breaching experiments** to test indexicality and disrupt people's common sense meanings, for example, sending his students to bargain for goods in shops when this is not a shared custom. He notes that an individual's use of common sense knowledge creates social order.

> ### EVALUATION POINT
>
> Ethnomethodology can be criticised as it only outlines the individual discovery of common sense knowledge. It could be suggested that this is something that exists beyond an individual as in the functionalist view of a collective conscience.

Phenomenology

Phenomenology looks at how humans use their senses to interpret what is happening around them. Schutz applies the individual's use of the senses to experience phenomena and explain how people categorise the world around them with others. He notes that meanings change based on the social context in which the actions take place. He sees people as having shared categories that they can organise experiences into called **typifications**. Schutz sees the world as **intersubjective**, stating that we must share meanings in order to coexist in harmony.

Structuration Theory

Gidden's **structuration theory** combines action theories and structural theories, arguing that action and structure cannot exist without each other. He sees that actions influence structures and keep structures dynamic, changing over time. He calls this relationship between actions and structures structuration. Giddens sees structure as made up of **rule**, the norms and values that influence actions and **resources**. He sees rules and resources as changeable over time although actions of individuals tend to simply reproduce the structures of society rather than change them. Giddens notes that in late modern society, where tradition is followed less, individuals are more likely to choose new actions, thus influencing the structures of society.

> ### EVALUATION POINT
>
> Some sociologists would suggest that Giddens fails to examine the ability of a structure to change an individual, instead he focuses on the individual's power to change structures, overestimating the impact of individual actions.

SUMMARY

- Action theories are a micro-level approach that takes a voluntaristic view of an individual's actions.

- Weber notes that sociologists should aim to discover the level of cause and level of meaning of actions.

- Weber notes that actions fall into one of four categories: traditional action, affective action, rational value-orientated action or rational goal-orientated action.

- Symbolic interactionism looks at individuals shaping the world around them, noting humans act rationally rather than instinctively. It sees individuals as giving meaning to actions based on social interactions.

- Goffman's dramaturgical model sees individuals as able to shape others' views of them using impression management when playing onstage roles.

- Labelling theory examines how people define situations as real, causing consequences to occur. It sees the concept of the self as a product of others' reactions.

- Ethnomethodology explains how a common sense knowledge is held by individuals and that indexicality occurs when this fails; reflexivity is needed to make sense of situations.

- Phenomenology looks at how individuals make sense of the world around them using their senses to experience phenomena. It sees experiences as placed into typifications.

- Structuration theory combines action theories and structural factors, seeing individuals as able to change structures in society.

QUICK TEST

1. What level of approach do action theories take?

2. According to Mead how are animals and humans different?

3. Which social action approach looks at how individuals experience the world using their senses?

4. Which term is used by Garfinkel to describe when meanings fail to make sense to an individual?

5. According to Weber, which category of action would be influenced by a person's beliefs?

6. Which sociologist sees the need to combine action theories with structural theories?

7. According to Goffman, what do individuals use to shape others' views of them?

8. Where does Cooley suggest an individual's concept of self comes from?

9. What do labelling theorists believe to happen when a situation is defined as real?

10. Which action theory looks at life as almost a play with individuals as actors selecting how to use the props around them?

PRACTICE QUESTIONS

Question 1: Outline and explain two action theories. (10 marks) **Spend 15 minutes on this response.**

> **HINTS TO HELP YOU RESPOND**
> Select any two action theories from Goffman's dramaturgical model: labelling theory, ethnomethodology or phenomenology. Note your response in two detailed PEEEL paragraphs. For example: One action theory is that of ethnomethodology. It studies how interactions in society make social order possible. Ethnomethodology assumes that individuals create their own common sense knowledge of the world around them that impacts on their actions. At times not all meanings make sense to individuals experiencing them and indexicality occurs; in order to re-establish the common sense knowledge, reflexivity must occur.

> **Item A**
> Social action theories see society on a micro-level, they examine the impact of individual actions on society taking a voluntaristic view of behaviour. There are a number of action theories that view behaviour slightly differently, from examining the impact of individuals on the structure of society to focusing on the typifications that individuals categorise their experience of phenomena into.
>
> Other sociologists believe action theories to be ignorant of the structural forces in society, neglecting to see the impact of sources beyond the individual.

Question 2: Applying material from Item A and elsewhere, evaluate the usefulness of social action theories. (20 marks) **Spend 30 minutes on this response.**

> **HINTS TO HELP YOU RESPOND**
> Start by using the item to explain the shared views of action theories, from the micro-level approach to the voluntaristic view of behaviour. Use Weber to explain how action theories can take into account structure. You can then use Giddens to suggest that structure should be taken into account further (possibly linking to functionalism or Marxism and the impact of institutions in society). Use ethnomethodology to explain how social order can be explained, evaluate this with the functionalist view of collective conscience and value consensus. Explain the labelling theory view that individuals are shaped by the actions of those around them, evaluate this with Goffman's view that individuals can manage others' views of them. Make sure that each point you make links to the question.

Sociological Theory: Sociology as a Science

Whether or not sociology is a science has been much debated. **Positivists** believe that sociology should take the form of a natural science; however, **interpretivists** believe that scientific methods are not appropriate for the study of humans.

Positivism

Positivists believe it is possible to use scientific methods to study and provide solutions for problems in society. They believe that reality exists beyond the human mind. Reality has laws of **cause and effect** that can be measured using **scientific methods**. These laws can be verified by gathering evidence to support theories; this is known as gaining **inductive logic**. This objective information can then be used to guide policy-making in order to improve society.

Quantitative Research Methods

Quantitative research methods follow the scientific process that positivists prefer, the **systematic testing** of a hypothesis in an objective and detached manner. Therefore they favour the use of official statistics, questionnaires and experiments.

EVALUATION POINT

The interpretivists' view is a direct evaluation of positivism and can be used to draw effective comparisons.

Interpretivism

Interpretivists state that scientific study using inductive logic is not suited to the study of humans. They believe an individual's **free will** makes the study of meanings that people attach to their actions a better method of understanding society. Therefore sociology cannot be a science because the laws of cause and effect fail to explain these meanings. Natural sciences fail to study **consciousness**, they are only useful for studying automatic reactions to external stimuli. People are not **passive puppets** to the forces of society and cannot be studied scientifically.

EVALUATION POINT

Points from the chapter on 'Sociological Theory: Social Action Theories' can be used to support the study of individuals.

Qualitative Research Methods

Interpretivists prefer **qualitative research methods** that do not adopt scientific methods in order to uncover the meanings people attach to actions. Max Weber notes that using **verstehen** (developing an empathetic awareness of an individual's actions) is key to the study of society; the natural sciences fail to do this.

There are two types of interpretivism, each of which views the study of society differently. **Interactionists** note that causal relationships can be found in society; however, these must come from the study of **individual interactions**, uncovering ideas through observation. **Ethnomethodology** and **phenomenology** suggest that society simply does not exist beyond the individual and therefore set patterns cannot be discovered.

EVALUATION POINT

Postmodernists support interpretivists in rejecting the natural sciences. They suggest that science is a **meta-narrative** (or big story) that explains some of the truth about human beings but not everything. They believe science is dangerous because it is frequently regarded as a fixed truth that cannot be disputed; for example, in explanations of the origins of life.

Falsification

Karl Popper is intrigued as to how science has become such a popular discipline. He disagrees with the positivist idea that science is based on inductive logic and that a theory can be proven by gathering evidence to support it. Popper believes science should be based on **falsification**, that a theory should be able to withstand being falsified through attempting to gather data to disprove it. He states that theories are provisional because they are only correct until they have been disproved. Theories that last a long time seem to be true because they haven't yet been falsified (despite their lengthy duration).

Popper proposes that sociological theories aren't scientific and therefore do not provide the absolute truth because it is impossible to disprove them by falsification. For example, the Marxist view that a proletariat revolution will take place can never be disproved as Marxists can claim that it is has yet to occur. Popper notes that sociology could be scientific if it produces hypotheses that could be falsified through **empirical research**.

EVALUATION POINT

Thomas Kuhn rejects Popper's idea that all scientists follow the same strict methods and are unwilling to look beyond the scientific paradigm.

The Scientific Paradigm

Thomas Kuhn suggests that science operates within a **paradigm**, a framework shared by a group of individuals. He notes that science works on a set of practices and routines unquestioned by its practitioners. Scientists are socialised to accept the scientific paradigm and without this shared view science could not exist. Popper notes that **normal science** remains unquestioned until **anomalies** occur, forcing the process to be questioned. This questioning creates a period of crisis from which a **scientific revolution** emerges when the scientific community accept changes to the paradigm based on new discoveries.

Kuhn argues that sociology is not a science because it is **pre-scientific**. It does not operate within one shared paradigm, instead there are a range of theories adopted by sociologists with several different views. Sociology could only become scientific if these differences didn't exist. He observes that science itself is not fully objective as scientists work within a paradigm that influences their thinking and values.

EVALUATION POINT

The idea that even within perspectives there is a lack of agreement supports Kuhn's view. Look at the chapter on 'Sociological Theory: Feminism' for an example of this. Note also the differences between perspectives such as Marxism and functionalism.

Realism

The **realist** view of science also differs from positivism. Realists try to uncover structures and patterns in society rather than gather evidence to support hypotheses. Sayar states that there are **closed systems** and **open systems** in scientific studies. Closed systems are studied in the laboratory where all the variables can be controlled. Open systems have variables that cannot be controlled and thus make it difficult to make predictions. Realists believe it is possible to explain open systems by looking at **underlying structures**. They claim sociology can be scientific as it aims to uncover structural forces in society and that this can be done systematically (as in the natural sciences).

EVALUATION POINT

The realist view can be supported by theories that study the impact of structures in society such as Marxism and capitalism, and also feminism and patriarchy.

SUMMARY

- Positivists believe that sociology should reflect the natural sciences, using scientific methods that gather quantitative data to discover laws of cause and effect.

- Positivists use inductive logic in systematic testing of hypotheses.

- Interpretivists argue that sociology is not scientific as natural sciences are unable to study consciousness and free will. They use qualitative methods including verstehen.

- Interactionists believe that individual interactions create causal relationships.

- Ethnomethodologists and phenomenologists believe that society does not exist beyond the individual.

- Postmodernists reject natural sciences, seeing them as a meta-narrative.

- Karl Popper believes that sociology is not scientific as its theories cannot be falsified.

- Thomas Kuhn sees sociology as pre-paradigmatic, lacking the required structure to be scientific.

- Realists note that even although it is an open system, scientific study can be relevant to society.

QUICK TEST

1. What is meant by the term inductive logic?

2. Which perspective sees science as a 'meta-narrative'?

3. What does Thomas Kuhn believe that sciences operate within that sociology fails to?

4. What do interpretivists believe that sciences are unable to study?

5. Which term describes the empathetic study of society that Max Weber promotes?

6. What type of research method do positivists prefer?

7. When does Popper believe natural sciences to be questioned?

8. What type of system do realists see society as?

9. What is meant by the term falsification?

10. What do positivists believe to exist beyond the human mind?

PRACTICE QUESTIONS

Item A

It is often debated as to whether or not sociology is a science. Positivist sociologists believe that sociology should reflect the natural sciences in order to map patterns in society to discover social facts. These social facts can be used to benefit society. They gather evidence to support their claims or hypotheses.

Other sociologists believe that sociology cannot reflect the natural sciences.

Question 1: Applying material from Item A and your own knowledge, evaluate the view that sociology is, and should be seen as, a science. (20 marks) **Spend 30 minutes on this response.**

HINTS TO HELP YOU RESPOND

Start by explaining the positivist argument that sociology can reflect the natural sciences, and use Item A to support this. Evaluate the positivist stance with interpretivist views that sociology fails to explain human behaviour effectively; this can be supported with action theories. Use Popper to explain that sociology is not falsifiable and therefore not a science; support this with a critique of Marxism. Note Kuhn's theory that sociology is pre-paradigmatic and this means that it cannot be scientific. You could also use realism and the concept that if science itself isn't scientific then why should sociology aim to be like a science?

Question 2: Outline and explain two theories that suggest sociology should not reflect natural sciences. (10 marks) **Spend 15 minutes on this response.**

HINTS TO HELP YOU RESPOND

Select any two arguments from interpretivism: Kuhn or Popper. Explain each in its own separate detailed PEEEL paragraph. For example: Karl Popper suggests that sociology cannot reflect natural sciences as he believes that sciences should be able to face falsification. He suggests that sciences often use inductive logic, gathering information to support their claims. Popper believes that it is more scientific to take a theory and bombard it with research that aims to finds flaws within it and thus falsifying it. Popper notes that sociological theory often fails to be falsifiable, making it unscientific. For example, Marxist views that there will be a proletariat revolution are difficult to falsify as Marxists could simply claim that the revolution is yet to happen. Popper believes that this makes sociology unscientific.

Sociological Theory: Objectivity and Value Freedom

All individuals in society have their own set of **values** and beliefs. Some sociologists believe it is possible to research society without the sociologist's values influencing the process and outcome. Others argue that sociologists can retain their own values but must detach themselves from them in order to remain **objective**. Some suggest that sociologists should actively apply their views to research.

Objectivity

Positivists believe that sociology should study observable phenomena to find the truth behind patterns in society. They believe that sociologists must remain **scientific** in their methodology. **Quantitative** research methods should be used to remain **objective** (free from influencing the study with the sociologist's values). Karl Marx believed the scientific study of society revealed what he saw as the **truth** of a society based on class inequality.

EVALUATION POINT

Many sociologists who studied trends in society (such as Marx with his idea that a proletariat revolution would occur) did so with the view that their scientific research would benefit society. This period of research is known as the **enlightenment project**.

Value Bias

Max Weber suggested that sociology should aim to interpret and understand social interactions. He felt that sociologists should aim to do this while remaining free of their own **value bias**. He noted that sociology was **value relevant** as this influenced the selection of research topic and methodology used. Weber believed that sociologists should be **value-laden** in interpreting actions, resulting in different interpretations from opposing sociologists with

differing values. However, Weber believed that once a concept was generated, social research could be objective.

Values are an integral part of the research process and can influence the research from when **concepts are operationalised** through to the recording of responses and **interpreting of findings**. Sociologists must also decide which findings are required in the **research report**, and this will also be the result of a process influenced by values.

EVALUATION POINT

Modern positivists argue that a sociologist's values should not impact on the research process at all.

Committed Sociology

Positivists in the 20th and 21st centuries believe that science is an objective process that looks at **facts** that are not subjective and do not change with values: therefore values are not relevant in social research. Gouldner believes that sociologists in the mid-20th century became too detached from their own values, with no moral awareness of the impact of their research or findings. Funding from governments and companies took precedence over the morals of research. Sociological research aimed to solve the problems that governments faced and was increasingly aware of the need not to criticise those who funded it.

Gouldner believes that a **committed sociology** should take place in which sociologists are transparent about their values and should state which side of a debate they are on. Gouldner notes the importance of values in creating a meaningful piece of research because they can often guide the research process.

Key interactionist Howard Becker believes that individual values influence social research. He notes that there is a clear division in the **sides** that sociologists take as a result of their values. With sociology being **politically aligned**, positivists and functionalists tend to take the side of powerful organisations in society (such as the government). Becker states the need to take the side of the oppressed (or **underdog**) in order to reveal the meanings that create their positions as an **outsider** in society. Qualitative methodology supports this in-depth discovery of meanings and is favoured by interactionists and interpretivists.

EVALUATION POINT

You can use labelling theory and its creation of outsiders to support Becker, or to examine the proletariat underdog at the hands of bourgeoisie oppression in a capitalist society. Gouldner takes this Marxist view in suggesting values in research should aim to end oppression.

Funding of Research

The **funding of research** is a significant cause of value influence on the process. It is important to examine who has funded a particular piece of research when examining its findings. **Funding bodies** may prevent the publication of findings that compromise them. Sociologists are aware of how their own research may impact on their **future careers** and ability to receive funding in future, and this also causes an impact of values on the research process.

All sociological perspectives involve values, from **Marxism** taking a **left-wing** approach, to the **conservative** views of **functionalists**. Individuals follow their own values in accepting which perspective they prefer. **Postmodernists** suggest that perspectives have their own **meta-narrative** (or big story) and no one perspective holds the truth. **Feminism** actively looks to challenge **patriarchy** and to effect change in society.

EVALUATION POINT

Use theory from crime and deviance, from families and households and also education to support the impact of values on sociology. Also look at social policy in the chapter on 'Sociological Theory: Social Policy' to see the impact of values of sociological research on society as a whole.

SUMMARY

- There is an ongoing debate as to whether or not sociological research should be objective or value free.

- Positivists see sociology as being scientific and believe that a researcher should use quantitative methods to reveal truths in society.

- Max Weber believes sociologists should remain free from their own value bias. He did, however, note that sociological research was value relevant and that sociologists should be value laden when developing concepts. Following this research can be objective.

- Values are involved in all parts of the research process from operationalising concepts through to deciding what to include in the research report.

- Gouldner criticised modern positivists as losing their morals in order to serve their funding bodies.

- Committed sociology suggests that sociologists should embrace their values and actively state which side of a debate they are on.

- Howard Becker notes that there is a clear division of sides taken in sociology and that the sociologist should take on the role of the underdog.

- Funding bodies can influence research as they can decide not to report findings that don't reflect their practices.

- Sociologists are aware that their careers could be jeopardised if they show extreme values in their research.

- Postmodernists see all perspectives as a meta-narrative and that no one value holds the truth.

QUICK TEST

1. What is meant by the term objective?

2. What is a meta-narrative?

3. Which sociologist believed sociology to be value relevant?

4. What do committed sociologists believe about values in the research process?

5. According to Becker, whose side should sociologists take in their research?

6. What is the enlightenment project?

7. Why should sociologists' careers influence their use of values?

8. Why did Gouldner criticise modern positivists?

9. How do the values shown by functionalists and Marxists differ?

10. What type of research methods do positivists prefer in order to remain detached from the research process?

PRACTICE QUESTIONS

Item A

Early positivists suggest that sociology should adopt a scientific process in which a sociologist is able to remain detached from their own values. Modern positivists see objectivity in social research as increasingly important. Max Weber noted that sociology should be value relevant, although sociologists should aim to be detached from the research process once they have identified a concept to be studied.

Other sociologists believe values to be integral to the research process and that sociologists should actively embrace values in their research.

Question 1: Applying material from Item A and your own knowledge, evaluate the view that sociological research should be value free. (20 marks) **Spend 30 minutes on this response.**

HINTS TO HELP YOU RESPOND

You should start by noting the view of early positivists and linking this to Item A. Then add Max Weber, noting that values are important in the research process yet sociologists should be objective when a concept is discovered. Contrast these views with that of committed sociology and evaluate this with support from Becker. You can select links from labelling theory to support Becker and his view that sociologists should take the side of the outsider. Note modern positivists and Gouldner's view of them being too detached from their research. You can support this with the impact of funding bodies and sociologists' careers on the values that they show. Make sure that each point you make links strongly with the question itself.

Question 2: Outline and explain two reasons why sociology should not and cannot be value free. (10 marks) **Spend 15 minutes on this response.**

HINTS TO HELP YOU RESPOND

Choose any two criticisms of objectivity in research from Gouldner to the impact of funding bodies. Make your points in two separate detailed PEEEL paragraphs. For example: The research process is heavily influenced by values. Funding bodies want research that supports their ethics and aims. A sociologist may be reluctant to show findings that compromise the funding body that they are serving. Funding bodies may omit any findings that misrepresent them from the research report. As a result it is impossible to keep sociological research free from values.

Sociological Theory: Social Policy

Social policies aim to address social problems such as hate crimes or racism. C Wright Mills (1970) stated that sociology should explain social problems and suggest social policies to solve them. Sociological problems are different to social problems, they are simply patterns or trends in society that call for a sociological explanation, and are not necessarily a problem for society. However, the two do occur together when a pattern or trend causes a problem in society.

Sociological Research

Sociological research into social problems is not always effective in influencing government policy-makers, although sociologists are often employed by government departments like the **Department of Education** to examine their effectiveness and influence future policies. However, sociological perspectives may not reflect the ideological stance of a government and therefore may have little or no influence over policy.

EVALUATION POINT

You can use educational policies that aim to eradicate sociological and social problems (such as the class gap in achievement) to support this view. You could also mention policies such as GIST (Girls Into Science and Technology).

Policies such as GIST aim to eradicate sociological and social problems.

Sociological Perspectives

Different **sociological perspectives** view the state and social policy in a variety of different ways. **Positivists** see sociology as scientific and able to uncover **social facts** that could be used to benefit society as part of the **enlightenment project**. **Functionalists** note that the state plays a key function in the **organic analogy** of society. Policy is important in reinforcing the **value consensus** needed in society to avoid **anomie** and can be used to fix problems in society. **Marxists** see social policies as creating **class conflict** and serving a capitalist class, rather than promoting equality. For instance, Slapper and Tombs see laws that provide health benefits for workers as capitalism showing a **caring face** and lulling the proletariat into **false class consciousness.** Marxists see policies that protect the NHS as serving capitalism by ensuring that a healthy workforce is ready to wage-slave for the ruling class. Marxists believe that sociology should aim to reveal the **true agenda** of social policies and their aims to support the ruling-class minority.

EVALUATION POINT

Marxists could be criticised for failing to note that policy causes gradual changes in inequality. It is evident that Marxists believe change will be radical and revolutionary and not achieved by policy changes. Marxists see other perspectives as tinkering with problems via policy – fundamentally, the key issue to be addressed is capitalism.

Social Policy

Townsend (1979) looked at how policy could change poverty. He created a model of poverty that examined **relative deprivation**. He proposed policy amendments that aimed to tackle relative deprivation, ultimately leading to the introduction of policies such as the **minimum wage** and **tax credits**, which aim to support those on low wages. This **social democratic perspective** aimed to redistribute wealth across society, it sees tackling poverty as the key aim of social policy.

Postmodernists like Bauman (1980) suggest that sociology should not have anything to do with social policy. They argue that an ordered society that can be explained through rational thinking does not exist and therefore no policy can be deemed as right in terms of aiming to solve social problems. Sociologists should instead focus on an individual's experience of **interpreting laws**. Bauman suggests that sociology should "show us how our individual biographies intertwine with the history we share with fellow human beings".

Feminists see state policy as reinforcing **patriarchy** and legitimising the subordination of women in society. The state reinforces the **nuclear family** by producing policies that promote marriage, for example **tax breaks** for those with spouses. However, policies have been influenced by feminist thinkers. Research by liberal feminists has led to policies that support **gender equality in education** and also **equal pay policies**. Radical feminists have impacted on social policies that ensure **refuge for women** who are victims of domestic abuse.

EVALUATION POINT

Despite liberal and radical feminist influences on social policy, Marxist feminists believe that the subordination of women in a capitalist society will not be changed by social policy: a **revolution** is needed to address this inequality.

The New Right

New Right conservative thinkers believe that the state should resist intervening in society. They believe policies introduced to support those experiencing poverty are detrimental. Charles Murray argues that the generous **welfare system** has led to a growth in the **underclass**, creating a **dependency culture** in which individuals have no desire for paid work and are willing to live off benefits. The New Right promote **zero-tolerance policies** that aim to influence a person's **rational choice**.

EVALUATION POINT

This can be supported with the right realist view of crime prevention (see the chapter on 'Crime and Deviance: Realism and Crime'). You could also use left realism and the Perry Preschool Project as a contrasting example. Other examples of New Right policy can be found in the education units (mainly in the 1988 Education Reform Act).

DAY 5

SUMMARY

- Social problems and sociological problems often overlap. Sociological research can aim to provide solutions to social problems.

- Positivists see social policy as the product of scientific research, which can be used to change society for better through the enlightenment project.

- Functionalists see social policy as reaffirming the value consensus and avoiding anomie.

- Marxists see social policy serving the interests of the bourgeoisie. Policies to support the proletariat are a display of the caring face of capitalism causing a false class consciousness.

- Townsend adopts a social democratic perspective, looking at policies to reduce relative deprivation.

- Postmodernists see perspectives that aim to make positive changes in society as meta-narratives. Sociology can only study an individual's experiences of policy.

- Feminists see social policy as reinforcing patriarchy. Liberal feminists have influenced policy in the education system and by the creation of the equal pay act. Radical feminists have influenced policies that support victims of domestic violence.

- The New Right see policies that provide welfare support as detrimental to society by creating an underclass and promoting a dependency culture.

QUICK TEST

1. What is the difference between a social problem and a sociological problem?

2. Which perspective sees other views that aim to benefit society as meta-narratives?

3. Which state policy may be seen as promoting the nuclear family structure?

4. Which group has risen as a result of the generous welfare state according to Murray?

5. What did Townsend aim to reduce with policy suggestions?

6. What do feminists see social policy as reinforcing?

7. What policies have radical feminists influenced?

8. Why do Marxist feminists see social policy changes as useless?

9. Which sociologist suggests that sociology should aim to "show us how our individual biographies intertwine with the history we share with fellow human beings"?

10. What type of policies do the New Right promote?

PRACTICE QUESTIONS

Item A

Sociological theories that follow the enlightenment project aim to find patterns in society that can change it for the better. Positivists believe that careful scientific research can be used to find social facts that can be used to influence social policy. Functionalists believe that social policy is positive in reinforcing the value consensus and allowing the state to serve as a vital function in society.

Other sociologists argue that sociology should have no links with social policy, as policies administered by the state only serve to support the wealthy minority in society.

Question 1: Using material from Item A and elsewhere, evaluate the views of sociological perspectives on social policies. (20 marks) **Spend 30 minutes on this response.**

HINTS TO HELP YOU RESPOND

Start by explaining the difference between a social problem and a sociological problem, explaining that they often overlap. Continue to discuss the positivist view of social policy, and support this with functionalism, making links to Item A. Evaluate the functionalist view with Marxist ideas that policy only serves the ruling class and that sociology should aim to uncover this. Note the New Right view of policy and the need for zero-tolerance impacting on rational choice; evaluate this using postmodernist views that the New Right argument is simply a meta-narrative. Make links to the question within each point that is made.

Question 2: Outline and explain two sociological perspectives on social policy. (10 marks) **Spend 15 minutes on this response.**

HINTS TO HELP YOU RESPOND

Select from any of the perspectives throughout the chapter and explain each in its own separate, detailed PEEEL paragraph. For example: Marxists view social policy as simply reflecting the views of the ruling class in society. They are a means of creating a further class divide, allowing the working class to develop a class consciousness. However, some policies seem to support the workforce; these tend to have a hidden agenda, for example, laws to support the NHS simply ensure that the bourgeoisie has a healthy proletariat to wage-slave for them.

Sociological Theory: Globalisation, Late-Modern and Postmodern Society

The sociology of the late 18th century consisted mainly of **modernist theories** such as **functionalism** and **Marxism.** These theories subscribed to the **enlightenment project**, that through scientific reasoning sociology can find patterns and knowledge that can be used to benefit society. This society consisted of **nation states** that had strict territorial boundaries and inhabitants who shared a common language and culture. Modern society tended to be **individualistic** as people were able to develop their own identities. It was a society built on **capitalist values** of competition.

Globalisation

Globalisation is the growing interconnectedness of people across the world; a blurring of national boundaries has occurred changing society dramatically.

> ### EVALUATION POINT
>
> Sociologists debate the effectiveness of traditional sociological theories to explain today's modern society and their relevance to a world experiencing globalisation.

The Reasons for Globalisation

Globalisation is the result of a number of factors. **Changes in the economy** have taken place due to increased trading across national borders and the growth of transnational corporations (TNCs). **Technological advancements** such as the introduction of the internet and increased international travel have improved global links. Sharing a mix of different cultures across national boundaries has increased the awareness of different values around the world. The rise of **political groups** active across many countries has also led to the growth of globalisation.

> ### EVALUATION POINT
>
> These changes in society cause debate among sociologists as to what type of society we now live in. Late-modern society? Or postmodern society? Late-modern society is a developed society that still accepts traditional sociological theories. Postmodern society is too fragmented and diverse for any of the traditional sociological perspectives to hold value.

Late-Modernity

Late-modernity theorists argue that today's society is simply an advanced continuation of modernity. They believe that the enlightenment project, subscribed to by functionalists and Marxists, is still relevant. Giddens observes people searching for **ontological security**. They need to feel secure, having knowledge of the world around them; however, social change has taken place and caused globalisation. By adopting **reflexivity**, seeing that tradition in society should no longer be a guide to behaviour, people have a **transformative capacity** to make changes to society. This causes instability.

Ulrich Beck states that late-modernity brings with it increased **risks**, which he claims are "spiralling away from human control". These are **manufactured risks** arising from **technological advancements** including, for example, nuclear disasters and global warming. Despite this **global risk**, Beck and Giddens believe it is still possible to achieve progress in society through the use of objective sociological reasoning, in essence still subscribing to the enlightenment project.

EVALUATION POINT

It is naive to suggest that individuals are able to respond effectively to global risks to change society for the better. Groups will always argue about which (shared) solution is best. For example, the political debate about the need for the replacement of the Trident nuclear submarine programme.

Postmodernity

Postmodernists believe that a new era of postmodernity exists in society. This is a dramatic shift from modern times and sociology needs new theories to explain it. Postmodernism emerged in the 1970s, in which individuals define themselves by what they **consume**, rather than their values. Postmodernists see the traditional sociological perspectives that subscribe to the enlightenment project as **meta-narratives**, each one an individual's version of the **truth.**

Postmodernity means that the enlightenment project is no longer achievable as there is no shared power that can improve society. Society is unstable with a lack of grip on reality. Baudrillard notes that signs created by the media have more meaning than reality itself; he describes this as **hyper-reality**. This uncertainty makes it impossible to develop a shared power to change society for the better. No one truth is possible.

In postmodern society people change their consumption of goods and adopt a pick and mix approach to their identity. This negates the traditional view of an **ascribed status** in society. This intensifies the lack of ability to see a shared truth and form a consensus about which theory or action is needed to benefit society.

EVALUATION POINT

Postmodernists fail to acknowledge trends in society that support traditional sociology, for example the class divide that supports Marxist views or patterns linked to gender and ethnicity. Postmodernists make a huge assumption, suggesting that individuals are unable to distinguish between actual reality and the hyper-reality created by media images. It can be argued that humans still use scientific knowledge to make changes in society that solve problems; advancements in medicine support this view.

Postmodern Marxism

The key Marxists Jameson and Harvey adopt some aspects of postmodernism in their thinking. They see the enlightenment project as still achievable. However, they do believe that society has entered a postmodern phase; this reflects the society that Marxism predicts being a new stage of capitalism on route towards capitalism's final epoch. They argue that changes in the production of goods, insecurity in the jobs market, and the growth of small independent businesses has resulted in **flexible accumulation**, a new way of making profits. This has caused political changes that provide a platform for oppositional movements like feminism. Jameson and Harvey believe that these oppositional movements have the power to change society for the better, retaining faith in the enlightenment project.

EVALUATION POINT

The acceptance of oppositional movements holding the power to effect change in society does not reflect the traditional Marxist view that only a proletariat revolution can cause change in society.

SUMMARY

- Sociologists debate as to whether or not society is in a late-modern or postmodern phase.

- Globalisation has caused debate over which phase society is in. It has come about by changes in the economy, technological advancements, the ability to adopt parts of different cultures, and the growth of new political groups.

- Late-modern theories still accept the enlightenment project. They explain change in society as a result of transformative capacity.

- As a result of technological advancements, late-modern society contains manufactured risks; despite this the enlightenment project can reduce these risks.

- Postmodernists believe that society is diverse and fragmented and that traditional sociological theories are meta-narratives.

- Postmodernity sees hyper-reality as causing uncertainty in society, impacting on the ability to change a diverse and fragmented society for the better.

- In postmodern society people define themselves by what they consume rather than their values, making it difficult to promote positive change in society.

- Marxists Harvey and Jameson see flexible accumulation as causing a growth in oppositional movements that aim to reduce inequality in society.

QUICK TEST

1. What type of society emerged in the mid-18th century?

2. What is meant by flexible accumulation?

3. In postmodern society, what do individuals define themselves by?

4. According to Baudrillard what has caused hyper-reality?

5. What do postmodernist sociologists describe sociological theories that subscribe to the enlightenment project as?

6. According to Beck, what has caused new manufactured risks in late modern society?

7. What are nation states?

8. How do the views of Jameson and Harvey about change in society differ from those of traditional Marxists?

9. What does Giddens suggest people share in order to be able to make vast changes in society?

10. What are people in modern society described as due to their ability to develop their own identities?

PRACTICE QUESTIONS

Item A

Sociology has long debated the stage of current society, from viewing society as being in a late-modern phase to society entering postmodernity. Postmodernists suggest that traditional theories of society are unable to promote positive change as they are simply meta-narratives that describe one person's version of the truth. They see society as too fragmented and diverse to adopt theories which change society for the better.

Others see traditional perspectives as still relevant to the study of society, noting that scientific rigour can identify cause and effect relationships that can be used to benefit society.

Question 1: Applying material from Item A and your own knowledge, evaluate the view that society has entered a postmodern phase in which traditional sociological theories are no longer relevant. (20 marks) **Spend 30 minutes on this response.**

HINTS TO HELP YOU RESPOND

Start by explaining the basics of the postmodern view. Support this with facts about globalisation and the scale of change in society. Evaluate postmodernity using late-modernity and the views of Giddens and Beck, and explain how these ensure that traditional sociology is still relevant. Continue on to note the postmodern views of diversity and fragmentation explaining hyper-reality and the confusion caused as a result of making the enlightenment project void. Evaluate this mentioning the naivety of postmodernists in suggesting that all individuals fail to see reality instead of media-created images. Use Marxist views of Jameson and Harvey to explain why the traditional view of Marxism is still relevant and evaluate this with the view that they reject the need for a proletariat revolution. Challenge the postmodern view that class/gender/ethnicity no longer matter.

Question 2: Outline and explain two characteristics of postmodern society. (10 marks) **Spend 15 minutes on this response.**

HINTS TO HELP YOU RESPOND

Select two notions of postmodernity, from hyper-reality to being defined by what we consume. Note each in its own detailed PEEEL paragraph. For example: Postmodern society consists of many media-created images which cloud an individual's judgement of reality in society. Baudrillard describes this as a hyper-reality where these signs mean more that traditional reality itself. The media places importance on these signs causing confusion in society. This confusion over reality means that people lack the ability to change society for the better as they are unaware of a true reality.

Media: The Impact of the New Media

The New Media

The new media is characterised as **interactive** and providing greater **connectivity** than traditional forms of media such as printed newspapers, television and radio. Digital media, and in particular **web 2.0** (interactive content) has enabled **user generated content**, promoting interactivity and connectivity; examples of this are vlogs (video logs) and individuals creating content for the internet. Commentators who are optimistic about the impact of the new media on society are referred to as **neophiliacs.** The digital media form enables greater consumer choice, higher quality produce and democratic participation. Douglas Kellner (2005) views the interaction that the new media encourages as a positive force that counteracts the concentration of power being held by too few.

EVALUATION POINT

Robert McChesney (2000) sees the growing domination of the new media by transnational corporations as a threat to democracy as they buy up successful businesses. **Cultural pessimists** like McChesney argue the new media is another way for the ruling elite to encourage consumer greed and they criticise its output of dumbed-down content.

The Public Sphere

Jurgen Habermas (1987) identified the **public sphere** as a place for free discussion open to everyone, which is good for the political health of modern democratic societies. The new media provides a forum via which the public can stop power elites forming through unscrutinised actions. According to Itzoe (1995) the new media helps mobilise people fighting against corrupt officials and/or immoral behaviour by allowing freedom of expression through protest and campaigning.

EVALUATION POINT

The assertion of minorities being heard and having a voice due to new media has been criticised because of the growth in digibabble (meaningless internet communication devoid of political or cultural significance); for example, the focus on **celebutantes** like Paris Hilton. The internet has also been criticised for giving extremist political and religious factions a platform upon which to publish their views as unchallenged facts. Greater consumer choice in regard to unfiltered content has led to fears that images of violence and pornography are accessible online. The internet is also vulnerable to criminal acts of sabotage like hacking, which can target individuals or organisations like banks and even governments.

The Impact of the New Media

Paul Anderson states that the impact of the new media can be seen in six ways. Firstly, **user-generated content** has increased leading to **citizen journalism** (the public recording news events and publishing them). Secondly, collective intelligence is combined through a range of resources to **harness the power of the crowd** (contributing their knowledge and wisdom). Thirdly, the generation of **data on an epic scale** contributes to the collective intelligence. Fourthly, there is an **architecture of participation** created by the involvement of its users. Fifthly, the value of **network effects** increases as usage grows (for example: Twitter). Finally, the internet operates in a spirit of **openness**, with contributors giving willingly and collaborating with other users.

Anderson ignores the **digital divide** that maintains the division between the rich and the poor. The poor are denied access to new technology because of its cost and also through lacking knowledge of how digital information is stored, transmitted and accessed. Boyle (2005) identified **convergence** as the process of creating a single delivery system that will force people to abandon analogue technologies because new devices will exclusively host business, consumer and social activity. For example, people will be obliged to do their banking online, or make payments using apps on their mobile phones.

Digital Corporatism Hypothesis

Shapiro's (1999) analysis that the new media will allow horizontal control (the mass audience) to replace vertical control (power held by the ruling elite) has been challenged by Medved's (1993) **digital corporatism hypothesis**. Medved contests that mega-corporations (such as Alphabet, Facebook, Sony, Viacom and News Corp) will colonise the internet and dominate it. Eventually this will lead to users paying to access websites. Also, rather than creating communities of shared interests, individuals will become increasingly isolated as they spend more time in the virtual world. Their online activity can be tracked, enabling companies to predict their tastes and target them; this leads to the individual becoming more materialistic (oriented towards things rather than other people). Herbert Marcuse's Marxist analysis in his work *One Dimensional Man* (1964) is a useful reference here: in modern societies consumerism creates the identity of the individual, and this is built on the desire of companies to make profits. As a consequently human relationships are undermined and societies are atomised.

Media imperialism stifles because of its overt influence in the global market. The largest companies prop up a small but very powerful group of people. This leads to the continuation of the practices that cause inequality. These companies operate unregulated. However, according to Negroponte (1996), choice will be broadened, freedoms greater and democracy strengthened by **digital liberation**. The virtual world does not require labels of gender, race or ethnicity. This represents an advance along with the end of censorship and copyright protection and the distinctions made between producers and consumers.

Hyper-Reality

Postmodernists offer some complex analysis of the new media. On one side there are those who welcome the unprecedented choices now available to individuals to construct their own identities (rather than living as prescribed). However, others like Baudrillard identify a less appealing aspect of the new media: what it tells us is real has become more of a reality than our own experiences (outside the sphere of the media). Images are captured and represented so readily and expertly that we cannot distinguish between them and reality. We live in a condition of **hyper-reality** (a distortion of reality). The **simulacra** (imitations) are indistinguishable from the original objects. Films, computer games and other online content contribute to the creation of the hyperreal. Within this virtual world the new media forces people to define themselves by the images they consume.

Strinati (1995) claims that this is a victory of style over substance, as we become slaves to branding. Critics argue that the influences of class, age, gender and ethnicity are ignored by this focus on signs and simulacra.

SUMMARY

- The new media is interactive, thus allowing for user-generated content (UGC).
- Neophiliacs are optimistic about the impact of the new media.
- Cultural pessimists view the new media in a negative light: it leads to even greater inequality as the powerful can dominate the new media for their own purposes.
- The internet is the public sphere; Habermas argues this is good for democracy.
- The internet has many negative impacts, it can provide a platform for violence, extremism and pornography.
- Paul Anderson's six points (user generated content; harness the power of the crowd; data on an epic scale; an architecture of participation; network effects; and openness) show the positive impacts of the new media.
- A digital divide exists, meaning that the impact of the new media is hard to measure across all groups in society equally (age and social class being important qualifiers).
- Medved's digital corporatism hypothesis pessimistically focuses on the transnational corporations that dominate and control much of virtual space.
- Baudrillard's concept of the hyper-real can help us understand the influence of signs and representations of reality substituted for reality; these simulacra may appear more real to us than our actual reality.

QUICK TEST

1. What is meant by a neophiliac?

2. Give two examples of the negative impact of the new media?

3. Which author described a place for citizens to participate in the political process as the public sphere?

4. What term is used to describe the public recording and publishing of news?

5. Which author notes six points or ways in which the new media or internet has impacted upon society?

6. What concept suggests that there may be very real differences of how the new media impacts on our lives dependent on social class or age or other economic factors?

7. Which author criticised the influence of consumerism in society, which has led to us becoming one-dimensional?

8. According to the digital liberation hypothesis, what will happen to copyright, gender and ethnicity in the future?

9. Which term describes the concept that we live at a time where reality is distorted by an overabundance of simulacra?

10. Who coined the terms simulacra and 'hyper-reality'?

PRACTICE QUESTIONS

Item A

It has been claimed that the new media differs from the old (analogue) media only in the speed at which it delivers content and that interactivity has always been present in the media through phone-ins, letters to the editor of a newspaper, and audience participation in TV shows. Cornford and Robins (1999), in addition to asserting that the new media is grafted onto the old media, are wary of any claims that the media enhance consumer choices and instead focus on the continuing power of the wealthy to dominate the new media and create artificial needs through targeted advertising.

Question 1: Applying material from **Item A** and your knowledge, evaluate the view that the new media has had a positive impact in society. **(20 marks) Spend 30 minutes on this response.**

HINTS TO HELP YOU RESPOND

Your knowledge of the pessimistic and the optimistic views of the new media should be demonstrated here. It may be a good start to develop the ideas given in Item A. State and define in detail the cultural pessimist view, and include the ideas of Marcuse and his work *One Dimensional Man*. These support the view of Item A that the new media is neither new nor beneficial to society. Your evaluation can be further examined by looking at the neophiliac viewpoint and go into depth about the benefits of this view as opposed to the digital corporatism hypothesis. Enhance your evaluation by exploring the ideas of Habermas on the public sphere and how the new media opens up new levels of participation in the democratic process. Do not be afraid to add in real life examples of your own use of digital or social media when engaging in politics or culture. Develop a sustained analysis by continuing to look at evidence both for and against the positive impact of the media. You can draw on debates surrounding the impact on children from other areas of the A Level course. Showing your understanding of the complexities of postmodern views of the media will help you reach the very highest level of marks. Do not be afraid to argue that the impact may be both positive and negative. Your conclusion should sustain the reasoning of your response.

Question 2: Outline and explain **two** ways in which the new media has changed the news process. **(10 marks) Spend 15 minutes on this response.**

HINTS TO HELP YOU RESPOND

Provide two clear examples and write a paragraph on each with some analysis of the point you are outlining and explaining. It can be useful to add a paragraph of evaluation at the end to show that you are aware of other important changes within the news-making process. A first example could be citizen journalism. Define this clearly and describe its impact on the news-making process. Also include ideas of news as a social construct. Be aware that often two topic areas can be combined within a single question and your answer should form a larger integrated understanding of both. Your next point could be the emphasis on consumer choice or interactivity shaping the news process and how this leads to a greater number of formats of news to choose from. Give examples such as 24-hour news coverage.

Media: Ownership and Control

The **traditional Marxist** view of the media (also known as manipulative or instrumental Marxism) is that the owners of the media control the content of the media. In this way the ideas of the powerful dominate. An elite view of the world is shown and accepted by a passive and uncritical audience, like puppets being manipulated by powerful media barons such as Murdoch and Berlusconi.

Cross-Media Ownership

Cross-media ownership means that one baron or owner has massive potential influence, power and control over the media. Rupert Murdoch has control of many media outlets in many countries.

> **EVALUATION POINT**
>
> **Ben Bagdikian** (2004) identified the **concentration of media ownership** into a few powerful companies as a threat to democracy. The **power elite** are the media barons, the political establishment, and powerful financial and industrial figures that seek to control how the audience sees the world. From this perspective the media has a powerful ideological function. Focusing on the powerful corporate ideology promotes a very conservative worldview.

The Power Elite

Editors are not able to exercise independent control or make objective decisions because they have to follow the guidelines set by the owners. Journalists owe their livelihoods to their employers and will therefore not challenge the conservative values that promote the values of the **power elite**. Conservative values support an unfair system that keeps a small minority (the capitalist class or bourgeoisie) wealthy at the expense of the majority (the working class or proletariat). Progressive ideas that would move society toward greater equality are not supported or aired by the media as genuine goals.

> **EVALUATION POINT**
>
> Pluralists would argue that there is a dynamic media market serving the needs of a variety of audiences because owners build their businesses on profit and not politics. **John Whale** (1977) found that *The Sun* newspaper was ailing until Murdoch transformed it from a left-leaning newspaper that represented workers' views to a newspaper that gave its audience what they want: sport and titillating stories.

Ideological State Apparatus

Neo-Marxists have adapted the manipulative or traditional Marxist approach to show that owners do not have direct control over their products but instead employ people who share their worldview (White middle-class men). These editors want to please their owners but will produce content critical of capitalism if it attracts audiences; audiences are not necessarily all the same. All the ideas produced by the media are within what is perceived as a moderate spectrum we perceive as being normal. The media, religion, family and education all form part of what Althusser called the **ideological state apparatus** that creates the common sense ideas that dominate. Here, Gramsci's idea of **hegemony** is important: where the ideas of the elite are seen as common sense ideas, their acceptance allows the rule of the powerful few to continue unchallenged. This control by consent means that any criticism of capitalism is perceived as being radical, dangerous or threatening to the legitimate and fair ideas of the hegemonic (dominant) class. A **false-class consciousness** exists in which capitalist ideas are shown as facts and failure to become successful within the capitalist system is attributed to the individual not working hard enough. For Miliband (1977) and Curran (2003) the shaping of public opinion toward a more conservative political stance is the result of the media's support of the power elite or capitalist class.

Nick Couldry (2007), in his report to the House of Lords, found that just six corporations control more than 90 per cent of the media output in the world and that their ideology does indeed influence the editorial process. Pluralists argue that the output of the media is dynamic, varied and challenging. Critical and investigative journalism can be found in many mainstream outlets (without even exploring new media channels).

Glasgow University Media Group has studied news output and found that controllers of the media set the news agenda based on the ideology of the owners. These media professionals won't contradict the ideas of the owners because they are from similar backgrounds and share a similar worldview. Martin Harrison (1985) found evidence of bias in favour of the establishment when it reported on strikes. Union leaders' views were not heard as often as the views of owners and bosses.

The Market Mechanism

Pluralists have taken their name from the works of **Jean Blondel** (1969). In his writing Blondel makes the point that contemporary societies are complex and do not permit the domination of any one particular group. Society is complex, with different groups (gender, ethnicities and social classes) all represented. In the media, too, no one group is dominant. The plurality of the media is guaranteed by the need to please audiences by giving them what they want. This is known as the **market mechanism**. The audience is diverse and chooses from a wide range of content shaped to their preferences; they are not puppets but are active consumers shaping content through their purchases, tastes and demands. Managers and editors make independent decisions based on their skills to create content that audiences want to buy so that owners continue to make profits.

The media is impartial and objective because it is diverse, free and interactive. There are regulations that ensure a balance of views. The media can be held to account through the laws of libel (untrue damaging content) and slander (verbal untruths). Ofcom was established in 2004 to regulate broadcasting. Journalists are trained to be objective in their pursuit of the truth and will investigate the behaviour of the power elite (for example, MPs' expenses scandals or tax loopholes utilised by the wealthy). The BBC, as part of a wide range of public service broadcasting, is viewed as serving the interests of impartiality and plurality.

Meta-Narratives

The **postmodern** view is not concerned with the relationship between owners and controllers. It regards the audience as active in using media images to shape their own identities. The media is important in the immersion of the individual in images or cultural signs. **Strinati** (1995) writes that postmodern theory analyses consumption patterns as sources of identity. Images are important in themselves rather than as symbols that carry deeper meanings. Postmodern theories have attacked meta-narratives (big stories) such as the idea that rational thought will lead to progressive improvements. Evidence such as the development of nuclear weaponry and the Nazi concentration camps are being used to support their attack on the idea that progress is always beneficial.

Jean Francois Lyotard is a key postmodern theorist seen as creating a meta-narrative of his own by identifying that we exist in a condition of postmodernity. The Marxist thinker Terry Eagleton regards postmodern theory as a justification for aggressive capitalism and thus inequality.

SUMMARY

- Traditional Marxists view owners as having total control of their media empires and through this control they manipulate a passive audience to conform to their worldview.

- Greater power has accrued to owners because of the concentration of media ownership through cross-media ownership.

- A power elite is thought to exist that is keen to maintain inequality; the power elite consists of very wealthy industrialists and business leaders and media barons.

- The neo-Marxist view takes account of the diversity of media output and shows it overwhelmingly from a safe, moderate and acceptable stable of ideas.

- Neo-Marxist ideas are based on Gramsci's idea of hegemony; he used this to show that the ideas of the ruling class dominate because they become legitimatised and accepted as common sense.

- The media is crucial in legitimatising ruling-class views or ideology by creating a false class consciousness (control by consent).

- Pluralist views see the audience as active in shaping the media through their choices (purchases); this is known as the market mechanism.

- Many structures exist to create a free media; some of these are legal (laws of libel and slander) and some institutional, such as the professionalism of journalists. This ensures the impartiality and objectivity of the controllers, editors and journalists.

- Postmodernists are not interested in the relationship between owners and controllers. The media is vital in shaping postmodern identities that are found within society.

QUICK TEST

1. Which perspective of the media sees the audience as puppets, easily manipulated by the content?

2. Which sociologist identified the concentration of media ownership in recent years as a threat to democracy?

3. Give two example of what Althusser called the ideological state apparatus.

4. What important concept does Gramsci use to explain how the ruling class continue to control the working class through gaining their consent to their worldview?

5. Whose ideas are pluralist views of the media based on?

6. What is the market mechanism?

7. How do pluralists view the relationships between owners and controllers?

8. What were Martin Harrison's findings on how the media portrayed strikes?

9. What theoretical viewpoint does Lyotard represent?

10. Why is Terry Eagleton critical of postmodern theory?

PRACTICE QUESTIONS

Item A

The Sutton Trust found that more than half of the top journalists had been privately educated. Privately educated people represent only 7 per cent of the population and can be said to have a disproportionate influence in the media. These journalists are editors or controllers setting the news agenda that the public rely upon to be impartial, fair and non-biased.

Question 1: Applying material from **Item A**, analyse two factors that Marxists argue can be seen to explain the relationship of owners and controllers. (10 marks) **Spend 15 minutes on this response.**

HINTS TO HELP YOU RESPOND

Start by explaining the difference between owners and controllers. The first factor can focus on the traditional Marxist view of the relationship between owners and controllers. Here the evidence of Item A would be useful to show how the content of the media is created to manipulate the audience's views of the world, the idea of agenda-setting could be unpacked. Use pluralist analysis to evaluate the views of Marxists, state that the audience is not passive but active and bring in ideas about the market mechanism to counter the idea of audiences as puppets manipulated by media barons.

Your second paragraph can focus on the hegemonic process. Again, this can be explained in tandem with the evidence of the Sutton Trust from Item A. Be detailed in exploring the ideas of ideological domination, control by consent, and false class consciousness. Evaluate these ideas with pluralist ideas of journalistic professionalism and the laws that ensure a free media.

Item B

Regulation of the media by Ofcom and the fact that the audience can hold the media to account by not buying a particular product are signs that we do indeed have a free media. Rules about cross-media ownership are another safeguard against one firm's dominance. Despite these claims, many who study the media's role in society believe it has an ideological role that benefits an elite.

Question 2: Applying material from Item B and your knowledge, evaluate the pluralist view of the media. (20 marks) **Spend 30 minutes on this response.**

HINTS TO HELP YOU RESPOND

You will have to examine a range of views on how the media operates. Define the pluralist view of the media, explaining the key ideas of Blondel. Explain the role of the market mechanism and be sure to show the negative views of the pluralist view using evidence from Althusser and Miliband (for example). Some of your essay will focus on the independent and objective roles of media professionals or journalists. Examine the Marxist analysis of the media and how traditional Marxists differ from neo-Marxists in their interpretation of the media. Postmodern views may be introduced to show how their focus is very different to other theories. You can use information from other chapters to show the breadth of your knowledge. Your conclusion will support your evaluation.

Media: Culture and the Media

In sociology **culture** is defined as the norms, values and beliefs of a social group. In this chapter we focus on the products of human relations, what the values and beliefs of social groups produce, specifically, in contemporary society, films and television programmes, literature, music, and the creative output of the new media. In the past it was thought there existed two distinct cultures: **high (or elite) culture** and **low (or folk) culture**. High culture was created for the wealthy, educated and literate minority. It relied on patronage of artists by the wealthy, a sponsorship of talented artists producing elite culture. The culture of the ordinary people developed from their own experiences and can reveal their values, norms and beliefs. Low culture includes folk music, crafts and stories. High culture is associated with fine art, opera and ballet.

The Pluralist View of Contemporary Culture

Two broad views of contemporary culture (or **mass culture** or **popular culture**) can be identified. The pluralist (and postmodern) view has a positive view of the changes in culture from the past to the present. Pluralists view the past as a harsh existence with little time for cultural pursuits. Nowadays everyone has **freedom of choice** and high culture is not reserved for the elite, it is accessible to all, resulting in a working class that are enlightened, more politically aware and better informed about the world. Although postmodernists do not view the past as any worse, they recognise that elite culture has become a **commodity** and is now used in a **pick 'n' mix** culture to shape our identities.

EVALUATION POINT

The Frankfurt School was a group of academics who studied culture and society to try and find reasons for the move toward totalitarian governments in Europe during the 1930s (the rise of fascism in Italy, Germany and Spain; the rise of a one-party state in Russia). These neo-Marxist intellectuals found that mass culture helped create mass societies by giving the **illusion of choice**. Marcuse (1964) wrote that "the hypnotic power of the mass media deprives us of the capacity for critical thought, which is essential, if we are to change the world". In a lowest common denominator (LCD) culture the audience is kept passive, compliant and silent. The media acts as the **new opium of the masses**, replacing religion as a drug administered to make us drowsy and not challenge the inequalities of society. We have become **one-dimensional** "people [who] recognize themselves in their commodities, they find there [sic] soul in their automobile" and other goods rather than in communities and relationships.

The Pessimistic View of the Relationship of Culture and the Media

A more **pessimistic view** of the relationship between the media and culture comes from the **romantic right** and the **radical left**. The romantic right thought that culture in the past was better: high culture offered the best that humanity could offer; artistically, philosophically and morally, elite culture improved human existence. Folk culture was authentic. Nowadays it is plastic. Folk culture once had traditions based on community but it has become mass-produced and uncreative. Leavis (1930) argued that the customs and traditions essential to secure social bonds were transmitted through folk culture. This has been replaced by an **Americanised culture** (detective stories, pop music and movies) that distort and/or coarsen human experience and so undermine social stability. In summary, folk culture grew and nurtured values that bound communities whereas mass culture (imposed from above) has corroded the values that once helped bind communities together.

For the radical left (the neo-Marxist Frankfurt School) culture was once dynamic, vital for social solidarity and change. Trade unions grew out of working-class communities and developed through a shared culture. Media has facilitated the isolation of people from their communities by the creation of a mass culture. They no longer pass on their experiences but consume a diet of trivia. They are distracted from their problems (in the real community) by being turned into what Marcuse calls "happy robots" in pursuit of "false needs". The higher living standards delivered by industrialisation and modernisation has turned them from **active** creators of culture to **passive** consumers of content. Cooperation through solidarity and community has been destroyed by selfishness, greed and the pursuit of commodities; these commodities are the hollow creations of advertisers marketing capitalism to the one-dimensional people that human beings have become.

EVALUATION POINT

Postman (1986) agrees with the negative impact of the media. In his analysis of television he notes that it appeals to the emotions and not the intellect. TV is good at entertaining, but Postman points out that the danger of this is that all content has been reduced to entertainment and is often transformed into "dangerous nonsense". Rather than being informed, people's emotions are triggered by news stories. These emotions are substitutes for opinions and this is why Postman decries television output as "dangerous nonsense".

Popular Culture

The radical left sees **mass culture** as creating societies where people are isolated from one another but kept happy through dumbed-down entertainment and titillating content. Individuals organise their lives through their consumption patterns. Pluralists do not agree with this and would suggest that **popular culture** (an interaction of mass culture with high and low culture) represents the spirit, morality, ambitions and intellect of humanity. Cinema has become a varied art form with a wealth of fine films. Popular music has also become varied.

EVALUATION POINT

The pessimistic views of right and left are critical of mass culture but differ because the right see the working classes as content to live in the past whereas the radical left view the working class as dynamic and organising themselves to make changes to society.

The Pick 'N' Mix Culture

The development of interactive technology has shown that people do want to be involved in the creation of their own culture and become adept users of the media, from which they benefit through a **pick 'n' mix culture**. Stuart Hall from the **Birmingham Centre for Contemporary Cultural Studies** (BCCCS) identified three ways of decoding the ideological messages of the media:

1. **Dominant** – uncritical acceptance by the audience of the media's message.
2. **Negotiated** – partial acceptance of the message; for example laughing at the comedic skill in an advert but not purchasing the product.
3. **Oppositional** – absolute rejection of the message.

EVALUATION POINT

Cohen (1972) and Willis (1976) have written about the complexity of the relationship between big business and youth culture. Big business seeks to exploit the products of youth culture as youth culture simultaneously repurposes items intended for mass consumption to create new cultural forms. The relationship between producers of mass culture and the consumers is complex, with a mix of rejection, adaptation and manipulation all present. Many argue that power still resides with the corporations or big business.

SUMMARY

- In the past there were two forms of culture: elite (high) culture of the literate and wealthy minority and folk (low) culture of the working-class majority.

- Pluralists and postmodernists have been linked to an optimistic view of the impact of contemporary or mass culture.

- Both the left and the right have been pessimistic about the impact of mass culture.

- Pluralists argue that there is now freedom of choice, with high culture accessible to all.

- Pluralists argue that there is a greater knowledge of social and political issues among all classes because of the way culture has developed.

- The right criticise the impact of popular culture as it destroys authentic culture. An Americanised culture creates junk tastes and gives no higher moral example to follow.

- The left criticise mass culture as it creates passive uncritical workers, destroys class solidarity or class-consciousness by replacing folk culture with a culture that encourages consumerism, individuality and greed.

QUICK TEST

1. Who was high culture produced for?

2. From where did folk culture develop?

3. Give one pluralist criticism of the way ordinary people experienced culture in the past.

4. How do postmodernists view elite culture today?

5. What was the Frankfurt School?

6. What did the Frankfurt School identify as "the new opiate of the masses"?

7. Which view argues that elite culture offered moral leadership to ordinary people, thus improving their lives?

8. Who argued that an Americanised culture had replaced the traditional cultures that bind communities together?

9. Which sociologist argues that television appeals to the emotions and not the intellect, thus having a negative effect on how informed about the world people can be?

10. What three ways of decoding media messages did Stuart Hall identify?

PRACTICE QUESTIONS

Item A

Through the media we can choose to listen to country music, reggae music or classical music. Corporations or big businesses are able to exploit popular culture to create vast wealth for themselves. Punk music and rap music, which have been seen as oppositional youth cultures, have become profitable forms of popular culture as huge media conglomerates have exploited these cultural forms.

Question 1: Applying material from Item A, analyse two reasons why people are critical of popular culture (10 marks) **Spend 15 minutes on this response.**

HINTS TO HELP YOU RESPOND

You must use Item A. Adopt PEEEL paragraphs. For example: As Item A states "huge media conglomerates" exploit cultural forms by reproducing them for mass audiences. Often it becomes a dumbed-down, lowest common denominator product; theorists from the left and the right have been hugely critical of popular culture as it is manufactured as a commodity to be sold. This means it is no longer born out of the experiences of those who make the culture.

This point must be evaluated. Use the optimistic view of culture put forward by pluralists or postmodernists. For example, if culture is now a commodity it allows it to be purchased by everyone, meaning there is greater choice. Your next point can be from outside Item A and could explore ideas of us becoming happy robots or one-dimensional, or the fracturing of community or social ties. Evaluate these points also.

Item B

Many sociologists have argued that the media has led people to be more isolated and so easier to control. The Frankfurt School has a very pessimistic view of the impact of mass media. Pluralists have pointed to the variety of culture that is on offer to everybody – folk culture, opera, sports, dance... There has never been a better time to exist if you want to experience the variety of culture available to all.

Question 2: Applying material from Item B and your knowledge evaluate the impact of popular culture on society. (20 marks) **Spend around 30 minutes on this response.**

HINTS TO HELP YOU RESPOND

Keep to the formula of the preceding chapter by stating both pessimistic and optimistic views of the impact of popular culture. If you are confident, outline the differences between mass culture and popular culture. Mass culture is a term often employed by those critical of the development of culture in modern industrialised societies. Ensure your chain of reasoning sustains the conclusion.

Media: Globalisation, the Media and Culture

Globalisation is the increased interconnectedness of the world made possible by the flow of ideas, technology, people and culture. The media has become a key component in the spread of information and ideas and the process of globalisation is a pivotal issue in sociology.

Cultural and Media Imperialism

Marxist analysis argues that globalisation has accelerated the domination of western norms and values and in particular American culture over other cultures. This process is called **cultural imperialism**, where the values of one society dominate others. **Media imperialism** has facilitated this because the largest media conglomerates are American-owned companies establishing the Americanisation of the world through the broadcast of a set of dominant ideas that ensure dependence on American cultural output (Fejes, 1981). Western cultural imperialism refers to companies controlling the manufacture and distribution of goods to the rest of the world through the establishment of **transnational corporations**.

EVALUATION POINT

The development of new media, digitisation and the impact of new technologies has led commentators to believe that a new era of global cooperation between people will develop. Governments cannot control the internet and this means greater freedom will be possible, facilitated by Habermas' idea that the public sphere will play a vital role in reinvigorating democracy.

Synergy

McDonaldisation or **coca-colonisation** are terms applied to describe the domination of western transnational corporations across the world facilitated by the major media conglomerates; these giant corporations are able to dominate markets by transforming people's tastes away from local goods to western (or American) products through **cross-media ownership** and the use of **synergy**. **Synergy** works (for example) by a company making a film, distributing it, then showcasing the movie in their cinemas. Furthermore they own the sports' teams who can promote the movie, and they own the rights to the music played in the film; this can be promoted through their publishing companies, radio stations and television channels. They can also work in partnership with the makers of bedding, clothing and jewellery to promote the film through a range of products, thereby employing at first horizontal and vertical integration then synergy.

EVALUATION POINT

Half of the world's economy is controlled by the 200 wealthiest corporations. Barber (1995) describes how transnational corporations are not limited by time and space. These corporations have become more influential in world affairs than nation states. Some believe that this is a deliberate strategy to dominate through cultural imperialism and others argue that these are the trends and consequences of a profit-driven marketplace.

Cultural Flows Theory

Cultural pessimists are accused of ignoring the reality of an increasingly multicultural world. To reach this level of hybridity of cultures there must be a flow of cultures not in just one direction but in all directions. This is what Tomlinson (1999) described as **cultural flows theory**. The homogeneous culture (a culture that doesn't vary) described by Marxists (and others) is actually a **heterogeneous multiculturalism** (varied by age, gender, social class and ethnicity). There are many examples showing how culture flows in several directions. One is Asian cinema, which has had a huge impact on western culture. Films ranging from horror to adventure to martial arts have found an audience in the west. The Asian film industry itself is diverse with Korean, Chinese, Japanese and Indian movies being particularly influential. Often these movies are remade in Hollywood; and actors from Asian cinema have become successful as a result. Directors like Quentin Tarantino have been influenced by Asian cinema. Bollywood integrates cultural styles from both the east and the west.

EVALUATION POINT

Gans (1974; 1999) has argued that there are no limits to the choices offered to audiences. His optimistic view of the impact of globalisation and popular culture is based on the fact that at no other time in history has so much diversity of cultural output been available to so many. Rather than culture being forced onto people, they decide for themselves based on their own tastes what they purchase.

Reception Theory

Cultural imperialism theories focus on the power of corporations to impose an ideology of aggressive capitalism on vulnerable economies (in underdeveloped countries). **Reception theory** rejects the idea that audiences are homogeneous and passive. Class, age, gender and ethnicity all inform the relationship between the media and the audience. Audiences are part of social networks where an individual's experience shapes the way media information is received by an audience. The media's messages are **polysemic** and can be interpreted in different ways.

EVALUATION POINT

Kennedy (2000) argues that local cultures are not subsumed by western or American culture. Local cultures adapt to the influences brought on them by the process of globalisation. Santos (2001) has examined the popular Mexican soaps that have a massive audience in the Philippines: these soaps are more suited to the values, aspirations and cultural sensitivities there than the equivalent American programmes.

Disneyfication

Disneyfication of the world's culture describes the American influence over global culture. American sitcoms and consumer products dominate and limit diversity of lifestyle or ideas. Putnam (1995) argues people become disengaged from their communities because of the time they spend watching television or using new media devices. These critical views can be linked to the cultural pessimistic analysis of the impact of globalisation, the new media and assessments of the impact of mass culture or popular culture.

EVALUATION POINT

Postmodernists point to the positive aspects of having all the world's cultural influences to pick from. Our national and gender identities and ethnicities are secondary to the influences of our **media-saturated** existence. We have globalised consumption habits and identities. For many the virtual world of online gaming or social networking have replaced the community of the places they live. TV soaps are substitutes for the lost relationships in local neighbourhoods. Awareness of multiple narratives creates sensitivity to a plurality of ideas, and older meta-narratives are rejected.

SUMMARY

- Globalisation is the growing interconnectedness of communities and individuals made possible by new technologies.

- Cultural imperialism is the domination of one nation's culture over another's.

- Media imperialism is the domination of one nation's media output over another's.

- Transnational corporations are mostly American-based and are vital in each of the processes listed above.

- McDonaldisation and coca-colonisation are terms used to describe the dominance of American culture over other cultures.

- Synergy is when businesses work together to promote products that are mutually beneficial; the media is often central to this.

- Cultural flows theory explains how culture does not move in one direction, rather influences from all parts of the world flow in several directions.

- Reception theory shows the audience is heterogeneous (varied) and interprets media messages actively (not passively).

- Disneyfication describes how consumption patterns of the world's population are tuned to American tastes.

QUICK TEST

1. The growing interconnectedness of the world is known by what key term?

2. The domination of one culture over another is known as what?

3. Businesses working together for their mutual benefit in marketing a product describes what key concept?

4. What theory is in direct opposition to the ideas of cultural imperialism?

5. Which sociologist studied the programmes dubbed into Filipino for broadcast?

6. What is reception theory?

7. What does the term polysemic mean?

8. How does Putnam explain why people are disengaged from their communities?

9. How have consumption habits become globalised according to postmodernists?

10. Why do postmodernists claim that we now reject meta-narratives?

PRACTICE QUESTIONS

Question 1: Outline and explain two ways in which the globalisation of the media has impacted culture. (10 marks) **Spend 15 minutes on this response.**

> **HINTS TO HELP YOU RESPOND**
> Supply two detailed points, evidenced and explained with the correct use of concepts. There are many points you could make, so tie them into your main idea; for example, write about cultural imperialism and the negative impacts that the export of American items is having on the more vulnerable economies of the world. Use key concepts such as Disneyfication and support these with the works of Putnam and Barber. Use your knowledge of postmodern theories to evaluate how globalisation can empower individuals to discover more about the diversity of culture available. Your second point could be an analysis of cultural flows theory, thus setting up a neat contrast of points that helps with your overall evaluation of the impact of globalisation. Provide a separate paragraph summing up your analysis to show your breadth of knowledge and understanding.

> **Item A**
> Satellite and cable television, digitisation, global advertising and the internet have led to the westernisation of other cultures. American food outlets like Kentucky Fried Chicken are found all around the world; some suggest this interferes with local cultures and changes people's tastes. Transnational corporations operate in a global marketplace in which powerful media companies advertise their products.

Question 2: Applying material from **Item A** and your knowledge, evaluate the effects of globalisation on the role of the media in society. (20 marks) **Spend 30 minutes on this response.**

> **HINTS TO HELP YOU RESPOND**
> Item A provides some direction although the skill is to show the examiner the depth of your knowledge and understanding of this topic. Evaluation is about debating the different views of the impact of globalisation. You should be aware that the media has an impact on the nature of globalisation, too. Defining globalisation as a concept or a process is a good start. The groundwork for this type of discussion is always between optimistic and pessimistic views of the nature of globalisation. You need to provide an in-depth understanding of cultural imperialism, link this to earlier chapters on cultural pessimism and Marxist understandings of globalisation, dominance and dependence. Perhaps your chain of reasoning will suggest that globalisation has been helped by media imperialism, or perhaps you can argue that the media has become more important as technologies have changed. Contrast the views of neophiliacs and cultural flows theory and reception theory in your response to help with your evaluation of cultural imperialism. Link sentences should read like this: The media has become more important as the effects of globalisation have become apparent. It could be argued that the extent of globalisation may not have been as great without the technological developments of the media. The same developments have been criticised for creating a global culture that is about sameness, whereas some postmodernists and pluralists argue that there is unprecedented choice for the consumer.

Media: Practical Factors Affecting the Social Construction of the News

The news is selective and its reporting does not show every incident. News is described as **socially constructed**. Decisions covering a range of interactions affect what the public view as news. Journalists and editors (**gatekeepers**) are powerful because they select what news items will be given to the public. For **pluralists** the news represents a **window on the world** and the news is an **objective** picture of reality. The gatekeepers have a power that is debated.

News Preparation

There are a vast amount of events that need structuring to fit the rigid demands of the different news formats. **Time and space** is a key factor for newspapers and television broadcasts. Complex stories have to be trimmed and their depth and context may be compromised. With cable television and the internet there are opportunities to develop news stories and run documentaries.

EVALUATION POINT

McQuail (1992) insists that the news is not a window on the world because it represents the interests, morals and worldview of the gatekeepers of the media. The news being produced is highly selective and a distortion rather than a reflection of reality.

Financial Constraints

There are **financial constraints** that influence the production of news. Print media has been affected by the rise of the **24-hour news cycle** and the new technologies producing news from a variety of sources. The cost of sending an investigative journalist abroad with a cameraperson and equipment is prohibitive. In the new media, news is streamed online and **citizen journalism** allows for user-generated content to be transmitted via social media channels. There still remains an audience for traditional news broadcasts and newspapers. The latter have become more dependent on **official sources** of information or **news agencies** such as the Press Association or Reuters.

EVALUATION POINT

Cuts to public spending have affected the BBC and events from around the world are not being given enough **depth of coverage**. Even prior to austerity, reporting on the Tiananmen Square protests in 1989 was so expensive for the BBC that inadequate funding was left to comprehensively cover the fall of the Berlin Wall the following year.

Advertising Revenue

Much of the revenue needed to fund a newsroom with reporters, editors and equipment comes from **advertising revenue**. Internet advertising reached £10 billion in 2017, in the UK as advertisers switched to mobile devices and advertised on sites like YouTube. The worldwide advertising spend was estimated at £466 billion in 2017, demonstrating the power and influence advertisers have over content. Advertising revenue from capitalist companies will not fund messages that are oppositional to capitalism and this skews the news content further. The political right and mainstream media are thought to benefit from the advertising spent by corporations.

Leadbetter (1998) has highlighted the very specific **advertising policies** of Coca-Cola in the positioning of their adverts in print media. Coca-Cola's adverts must not appear adjacent to articles containing hard news, sex-related issues, prescription drugs or medicine for treating chronic illnesses such as cancer, diabetes or AIDS, mental or physical medical conditions, negative diet information (for example, bulimia, anorexia or quick weight loss), food, political or environmental issues, articles containing vulgar language or religion. This is not a direct policing of the editorial policies of individual magazines but does potentially constitute a direct influence on their content. Other large companies have similar policies in place according to Leadbetter's findings. Coca-Cola spent over £3 billion on advertising in 2016.

The Digital Revolution

Even before the **digital revolution** a diversity of media content could be found and a range of views given. For example, Mark Thomas' *Comedy Product* was a critical and investigatory programme that researched Coca-Cola and GCHQ. The rise of digital media has meant that series like *The Young Turks* and Russell Brand's *Trews* have added critical voices to more mainstream news content like *Al Jazeera News* (privately financed) which aims to provide balanced, in-depth analysis and reporting from around the world.

News Management

News management is a technique politicians use to apply **spin** to news content, showing a particular group, event or view in a more favourable light. Politicians and journalists become partners in managing news stories, with journalists aware that they will lose access to the politician if they are not compliant. According to Franklin (1997) the news has become more about entertainment and is no longer part of an arena of informed debate but part of the **infotainment** industry. In this environment celebrity journalism replaces investigative reporting.

Marxists suggest that capitalism goes unchallenged because even when politicians face questions they don't inform the political debate but confuse it by focusing on personalities.

News Values

Schleissinger (1978) maintains news is planned in advance and that its gatekeepers plan news based on a **news diary**. The decision to attend and report political gatherings and demonstrations is made well in advance. **Value judgements** are applied to the news based on broader **news values** that journalists are socialised to have an understanding of.

News values are important in shaping value judgements about what is **newsworthy**. These are informal criteria guiding which stories should be given prominence. Galtung and Ruge (1965) list: frequency, threshold (the size of the event), unambiguity, meaningfulness (cultural proximity, relevance), consonance (what the audience expects and demands as news), unexpectedness (unpredictability, scarcity), continuity (part of the cycle of newsworthiness), composition, reference to elite nations (a story has greater importance if it involves UK citizens or Europeans), reference to people from the elite (ordinary people are deemed not newsworthy), reference to personalities (complex stories deconstructed so they are easier to understand), reference to something tragic (for example, a famine). A mixture of these values gives an item a better chance of being published or broadcast; the application of news values varies in each organisation.

SUMMARY

- News is a social construct shaped by a range of factors, it is not a window on the world.
- Gatekeepers (journalists and editors) are powerful in the social construction of the news.
- Pluralists see the news as a virtual window on the world; journalists report objectively on reality.
- Time and space, financial concerns and news management are constraints on producing value-free objective news.
- Advertising revenue can influence news content, as the money of big corporations with particular interests and world views keep those news media in operation.
- News diary – the news is planned in advance and so can be open to undue subjective influence or the values of a newsroom.
- News values are important in shaping news content based on determining what is newsworthy.
- The digital revolution keeps journalism competitive, varied and free of undue political influence.
- News management has led to a dumbing down of content, the rise of spin and personality over serious political debate.

QUICK TEST

1. Who are the gatekeepers?

2. Which theoretical view describes the news as a window on the world?

3. Name a news agency.

4. What was the estimated expenditure on advertising globally in 2017 set to reach?

5. Who has drawn attention to the advertising policies of big companies?

6. What word is used to describe the deliberate management of the news by politicians?

7. What is the function of the news diary?

8. Who describes the news as being transformed from investigation to infotainment?

9. How is the newsworthiness of a story calculated?

10. Which theoretical view argues that the news is often reduced to personalities, avoiding in depth analysis of the issues?

PRACTICE QUESTIONS

Item A
It can be argued that the news is a virtual window on the world. Others point to the power of the gatekeepers in determining what becomes news. Some would say that many factors determine what becomes news, such as the news diary or news values.

Question 1: Applying material from **Item A**, analyse **two** factors that impact the selection of newsworthy stories. **(10 marks) Spend 15 minutes on this response.**

HINTS TO HELP YOU RESPOND
Select two factors that are linked directly to Item A. In it we are given the information that journalists are neutral and objective: link this to the pluralist view and to the term window on the world. Evaluate this phrase using McQuail's criticisms of the controllers (gatekeepers) having a particular and subjective world view they cannot detach themselves from. You should include a range of concepts to support your evaluation of one factor. Another factor can be the news diary or the cycle of newsworthiness (news values). Evaluate this by using the evolution of news in the age of citizen journalism and social media or by enlisting Franklin's criticism of news as infotainment.

Item B
Some sociologists have shown that the processes affecting the selection and presentation of the news are far from objective. A range of factors has been shown to influence the shaping of what the audience trust as factual news content. With the growth of fake news and the questioning of journalistic integrity by the public, some are concerned that democracy may be damaged by a lack of trust in the balanced news that does exist.

Question 2: Applying material from **Item B** and your knowledge, evaluate the view that the news is a social construction. **(20 marks) Spend 30 minutes on this response.**

HINTS TO HELP YOU RESPOND
Read Item B carefully and note the different viewpoints expressed in it. Item B may illustrate a natural tension for your own essay, a set of opposing views you can explore in your evaluation. You can start with a clear definition of how the news is the product of particular cultures, times and places, it has to be a social construct by the very nature of the process of selection and the application of news values to determine what is a newsworthy story. Remember to write in depth on a range of points that show how the news is constructed: news diary, financial constraints, time and space. Evidence these with clear examples and evaluate using Item B (for example, by resisting the notion that these practical factors encourage fake news because the pluralist view highlights journalistic integrity and professionalism). Further evaluate this with the Marxist view.

Media: Ideological Factors Affecting the Social Construction of the News

Ideological State Apparatus

The Marxist view of news is that it is used to transmit the world view or ideology of the ruling class. Thus the news is tailored to suit a particular view of the world and so must be biased. The owners of the media employ gatekeepers who share their ideological views. The gatekeepers are White middle-class men who are rewarded for maintaining the **hegemony** of the ruling class, and they adhere to the newsroom culture dictated by the owners' capitalist ideology. Althusser states that news media is part of the **ideological state apparatus**, the function of which is to create **false-consciousness** among the working classes.

EVALUATION POINT

Pluralists make a clear distinction between news reportage and comment. Journalists remain impartial when reporting news events although they will summarise the comments of others to give a balance of views. The gatekeeping process is not biased or influenced by a particular world view. Consumers have a range of media to choose from. New media empowers the public to select news stories via social media channels.

Churnalism

Neo-pluralism describes the views of Nick Davies as outlined in his book *Flat Earth News* (2008). Like pluralists, neo-pluralists believe journalists are impartial and objective professionals pursuing facts. However, the modern journalist faces barriers in pursuing these facts. Journalism has become **churnalism**, with journalists over-dependent on the information provided by public relations' experts and spin doctors working for elected officials. Journalists produce news stories without fact-checking. The barriers to fact-checking are the rush to meet deadlines and competition with other news platforms to be the first to break news stories while having fewer resources at their disposal. Davies argues that journalists have lost sight of their objectivity and operate in a "professional cage that distorts their work".

EVALUATION POINT

Marxists disagree with Davies' claim that journalists strive for objectivity and neutrality in their profession. McChesney (2002) argues that the media presents itself as unbiased or apolitical because it helps disguise that the media is a corporate monopoly focused solely on profit. Journalism as value-free and impartial observation of events is an **ideological myth**.

The Power Elite

Bagdikian warns of the dangers of the **concentration of media ownership**. His fear is that democracy is not served by allowing a few powerful corporations to dominate the news media. The owners of these firms are part of a wider **power elite** that represents industrialists, the military and political establishment. This power elite serves only the interests of the powerful at the expense of the wider populace. It delivers a conservative **news agenda** serving corporate values.

The freelance journalist Monbiot (2004) echoes the criticisms of Davies and Bagdikian and states that the news reproduces falsehoods (for example, these lies led to the invasion of Iraq in search of weapons of mass destruction that never existed).

The neo-pluralist Davies and Marxists are critics of the news media. Neo-pluralism differs from Marxism because it hopes to recapture a time when a journalist was given the time and financial backing to uncover a story. Davies was inspired to become a journalist by the journalists who uncovered the Watergate scandal, which brought about the downfall of President Nixon.

Ideological Bias

Herman and Chomsky (1988) argue that the media **manufacture consent** by investing time and energy in propaganda that supports the elite. Edwards and Cromwell (2006) stress that the media act as guardians of power, shielding the cost of corporate crimes (pollution, genocide, the sponsorship of military coups) from the public.

The **ideological bias** of the media is fundamental and pervades the language of news itself. Claude Levi-Strauss described how **binary oppositions** are used in language, with one of a pair of values being reported negatively. The Glasgow University Media Group (GUMG) analysed the reporting of strikes using **semiotic analysis** and noted that managers were described as making "offers" while striking workers made "demands". In this binary opposition the strikers are portrayed negatively in the relationship and the managers are cast as positive, conciliatory, rational and sensible. Thus semiotics, the study of signs, can reveal the hidden connotations of text and images.

The GUMG explain the conservative nature of news content with reference to the **social background** of professionals who profit from the continuation of a system that benefits them as White, middle-class gatekeepers. They have nothing to gain from change and nothing in common with the poor and powerless in society.

Schlesinger (1990) finds it difficult to support theories of a unified power elite as companies are in direct competition with each other for profits. They operate within democracies and have to be mindful of public opinion.

Primary Definers

Stuart Hall has identified a **hierarchy of credibility** in which the powerful have better access to the media because they are seen as credible or expert in adding comment and analysis to news. These **primary definers** (as Hall describes them) are given more media time to outline their views than union leaders or others involved in the events that make the news. Primary definers make good spin doctors because journalists present them as trustworthy and impartial, yet they often have a hidden agenda (to gain public support for government policy). **Moral panics** often use primary definers to persuade the public to support the ideology of the ruling party. Many believe that moral panics are also a way of increasing profits by selling more news.

Pluralists argue that there is so much diversity with new media that Couldry's (2007) allegation of an imbalance of corporate-owned media affecting the democratic process is an exaggeration. Even bloggers have to obey the law to avoid being charged. **The Leveson Inquiry** (2011) provides proof that the news media is under scrutiny in the UK. The inquiry investigated *News of the World* journalists involved in **phone hacking**. The inquiry condemned the actions of the journalists found guilty and appraised the role of **self-regulation** of the press by the **Press Complaints Commission (PCC).** It was decided that the government should not regulate the press but that self-regulation should be enforced through legal measures. Many felt government involvement in regulating the press would curb the ability of the press to properly scrutinise those in power. Hodkinson (2012) argues that the press, police and government have operated together to harm and not help the British public.

SUMMARY

- Marxists believe that gatekeepers are well rewarded for maintaining the dominance of the ruling-class ideology.

- Althusser identifies the media as an important part of the ideological state apparatus that ensures false class consciousness.

- Pluralists view journalists as impartial professionals presenting the facts objectively.

- Neo-pluralists state that journalists face obstacles in pursuing the facts. They have too few resources and not enough time to check their facts.

- Churnalism is the product of a lack of fact-checking, as journalists have become reliant on the information passed to them by spin doctors and public relations' companies.

- Neo-Marxists such as McChesney argue that the view of the impartial and professional journalist is an ideological myth. It distorts the true reality that journalists work for the capitalist system to maximise profits by selling a particular lifestyle.

- Herman and Chomsky view the media as actively partaking in propaganda campaigns to support the power elite.

- Stuart Hall identified a hierarchy of credibility that works to authenticate the voices of the powerful as primary definers while devaluing the experiences of those without power.

- There has been a debate around the freedom of the press with a long-running inquiry (the Leveson Inquiry) recommending measures to make self-regulation effective.

QUICK TEST

1. What barriers exist to prevent journalists delivering the facts to the audience?

2. According to neo-pluralist thinking, what type of journalism has an over-reliance on spin doctors and public relations' companies created?

3. Who said that journalists "operate in a professional cage that distorts their work"?

4. Whose news agenda is served by today's media according to Bagdikian?

5. Who argues that the news reproduces falsehoods such as stories claiming that Iraq had weapons of mass destruction?

6. What crimes are the power elite covering up through their manufacture of news content according to Edwards and Cromwell?

7. What is the concept that explains how language is used to shape meaning through the uses of positive and negative attachments of value?

8. According to the GUMG, what is the root cause of the conservative nature of news output?

9. In Stuart Hall's hierarchy of credibility what is the name given to the powerful?

10. What was the cause of the Leveson Inquiry ?

PRACTICE QUESTIONS

Question 1: Outline and explain **two** ways in which the interests of the powerful are thought to be supported by the news. **(10 marks) Spend 15 minutes on this response.**

HINTS TO HELP YOU RESPOND

Although this question can be read as criticism that Marxists make of the way news is constructed you can also use the criticisms of Davies and his ideas on churnalism. Several factors are identifiable. Choose two: concentration of media ownership (Bagdikian, Couldry) is one, and link this to the question. Concentration of media ownership ensures that corporate (capitalist) values are supported in the news media. The news media may censor themselves by omission of stories that damage the image of corporations. Analyse this by distinguishing it from the pluralist ideas (Schlesinger). Your second point can be based on Davies' ideas of the professional cage that distorts the work of journalists. Explain the pressures of modern journalism and the shift to infotainment over investigation. Analyse your points in a concluding paragraph to add depth. For example, include detail on regulatory laws or the impact of the new media that ensures a competitive, free media to exist.

Question 2: Using material from **Item A** and your knowledge, evaluate sociological views of the selection and presentation of the news. **(20 marks) Spend 30 minutes on this response.**

HINTS TO HELP YOU RESPOND

Selection is obviously referring to the news as a social construct (or not), so be prepared to define this concept and examine the different theoretical (sociological) views: pluralist, neo-pluralist, Marxist (Bagdikian, Monbiot, Chomsky, Althusser, McChesney). Your evaluation will be weighing the case for a corporate-influenced media (with too much concentration of ownership) versus the active audience choices available (especially in the age of the new media and the development of citizenship journalism, vlogs, blogs and other social media forms that provide instant access to newsworthy stories). Presentation is at the same time wrapped up in and distinct from selection; think about Stuart Hall's use of the hierarchy of credibility in inviting the audience to trust some sources over others. This ties into the idea that journalists themselves are objective and provide a window on the world. Show your knowledge and understanding of the range of reasons given as to why the news is thought of as a social construct. This ties in with selection and presentation and with the idea of the distortion of reality.

Media: Media Representations of Gender and Ethnicity

The oversimplification of the characteristics of certain groups by the media has led to accusations of **stereotyping**. These generalisations have led to **labelling** of certain groups in society.

Binary Oppositions

Many studies of how the media represent masculinity and femininity have discovered that they reinforce stereotypical gender roles, norms and values. One way in which this is achieved is through the use of **binary oppositions**. Men are represented as strong and assertive while women are weak and yielding. In western societies it is the male that is seen as positive.

The kinds of binary oppositions that **Levi-Strauss** analysed were supportive of the feminist analysis of the representation of women in the media. The media reinforced patriarchal power, the authority and power that men have over women in society.

EVALUATION POINT

L van Zoonen (1994) argues that successful women in the media have to accept the **patriarchal ideology** that exists in structures within media companies. Liberal feminists argue that the imbalance in the representations of gender can be challenged once women are in positions of power. Radical feminists still point to the sexualised images of women in adverts as a sign of women's continued subservience.

Symbolic Annihilation

Gaye Tuchman's analysis of the media based on the effects approach found that women's achievements were secondary to their looks or sex appeal. In media portrayals successful women were **absent** (too few roles); or they were **trivialised** (no powerful roles) or **condemned** (betraying men; morally suspect). This led to their **symbolic annihilation**. Tuchman's work was published in 1978. At that time Tuchman found that women were outnumbered by men three-to-one on television. Men were the authority figures, presenting panel and discussion programmes and appearing as breadwinners and powerful leaders. When women did appear they were restricted to romantic or sexual roles, or roles as housewives and homemakers.

EVALUATION POINT

Changes took place in the 1980s. Abercrombie (1998) notes the rise of soaps featuring strong female characters with storylines driven by these characters. This change can be seen as revolutionary as women who were peripheral moved centre-stage. Others challenge this, arguing that women were still displayed for the **male gaze**. Laura Mulvey's (1975) concept explains why the camera lingers on the female form: it is because programmes are constructed from a male perspective and thus establish the voyeuristic pleasures of powerful heterosexual males. Winship (1987) finds that women's confidence and assertiveness is presented in magazines that tackle taboos.

The New Woman

Depictions of women in the 1990s show a more assertive and ambitious image being conveyed by the **new woman**. The Policy Studies Institute (1999) analysis of women's magazines described women as vain, consumerist and sexually assertive, with confidence in the social world.

EVALUATION POINT

Marxists claim the changes represent a move to capitalise on the potential opportunities for profit provided by a growing number of economically independent women. Advertisers want to capture the spending power of this growing audience.

Reception Analysis

Active audience approaches and **reception analysis** examine what the audience do with the media, how they interpret messages in a variety of ways. Radway (1984) found that women who read romantic fiction did so to find a space of resistance from the patriarchal structure of their everyday lives.

A **cult of femininity** was developed by magazines. Traditional ideals of women as carers, basing their lives around marriage and family, means serving others and maintaining their beauty and slim body for their husbands. Wolf (1990) defines this as the **beauty ideal**, continually striving for perfection. This is different to Mulvey's analysis, which concludes that women are objectified by the media – they become **sex objects.**

Metrosexual Males

Representations of males have followed a similar path, with **metrosexual males** (sensitive men who care about their looks) being condemned as the product of advertisers or explained by changed social attitudes.

Othering

Othering is a process by which people are subordinated, excluded or locked out of society. Jones and Jones (1999) have identified that Black actors are cast as aliens in films and on TV to reinforce their perceived essential difference. **Othering** creates a sense of national identity based on differences, helping to segregate and support the wider narratives of news stories. Van Dijk (1991) found flattery and self-deception supported a distorted ideology of British national identity laced with notions of superior British values that masked racist and reductive explanations for inner-city riots.

Minority culture has become mainstream culture. This has helped with positive portrayals of ethnic minorities. Abercrombie (1996) points to the less stereotypical characters in television as a sign of change. Ethnic minorities have championed media themselves (TV, magazines). The development of the new media has impacted significantly by offering choices.

Pluralists state that these representations are based on the actual positions of ethnic minorities in predominantly White societies. Like functionalists they emphasise the appearance of positive racial stereotypes within the media. The media is reflecting mainstream (White) opinions and values in its portrayal of minority ethnics, but this is not new. Ligali (2008) found that Black victims of crime do not get the same coverage as White victims; the plight of one White British person is magnified while the plight of thousands of foreigners is diminished by the imbalanced coverage.

Tokenism

Hall (1989) found that the western superior White culture is played out through the stereotypes of Black people as **natives**, **entertainers** and **slaves**. The White eye denigrates Black people as troublemakers, and there is often a token Black character: a **gangsta**, **criminal** or **drug addict**. More recently Black characters are shown as succeeding in sectors where intellect is secondary to physical attributes.

Pluralists and postmodernists maintain that audience choice and their active participation in interpreting media texts mean that these stereotypes do not have the power they once had. The fear of Muslims (Islamophobia) has been put down to stereotyping or the huddling together of Muslims by Dr Haideh Moghissi. There must be a recognition of the multicultural media that is available.

Coup-War-Starvation Syndrome

Coup-war-starvation syndrome reinforces myths about Africa. The government report *Viewing the World* (2000) identified a bias in reporting that shaped public perception of African countries as lacking competency, being corrupt, or the populace being lazy and having too many babies. These perceptions simultaneously cast the British as the only people able to sort these problems out through Comic Relief or Live Aid. These ideas support the notions about White western superiority.

SUMMARY

- Stereotyping leads to labelling and the media is believed to contribute to this process.
- Men are given the positive qualities when binary oppositions are in play.
- Feminists believe that a patriarchal ideology still shapes the media and women are subservient in this structure.
- Symbolic annihilation occurs by the absence, condemnation and trivialisation of women in the media.
- Laura Mulvey's concept of the male gaze leads to the objectification of women.
- Changes to the portrayal of women does not mean the cult of femininity is lost.
- Active audience approaches show that the message is not always interpreted as the makers mean it to be.
- Minority (non-White) ethnic groups are denigrated by the media while White western (British) values are celebrated.
- Othering reinforces nationalistic ideas of difference and separateness by portraying Black peoples as aliens in films and television.
- Coup-war-starvation syndrome summarises the reductive portrayal of African countries, from which the public believe Africans are responsible for their own problems but need British people to help them solve their problems.

QUICK TEST

1. How does the process of symbolic annihilation operate?

2. What theorist created the idea of the male gaze to analyse how women are portrayed by the media?

3. Females are now part of the cast of characters of soaps, driving plot lines, essential to the stories being told. Which author identifies this trend?

4. Which perspective explains the changed representations of women in the media as being explained by a search for new markets and profits as a way to capitalise on these changes?

5. Which method of research has replace effects methods?

6. What is meant by the cult of femininity?

7. How does the process of othering operate to diminish, separate and exclude groups of people?

8. What does Ligali identify as a concern with news reporting of crime?

9. In what three ways does the western media portray Black people?

10. Which sociologist describes the media's treatment of Muslims as leading them to being portrayed as huddled together within society?

PRACTICE QUESTIONS

Item A
There are increasing numbers of positive role models for women in the media. The economy has become feminised in recent decades. Society has felt the impact of a genderquake, women prioritising economic success over family. This means that women are no longer portrayed as sex objects in the media or solely as housewives and mothers.

Question 1: Applying material from **Item A**, analyse two factors that lead to the portrayal of women in stereotypical roles. (10 marks) **Spend 15 minutes on this response.**

HINTS TO HELP YOU RESPOND
Firstly explore the stereotyping of women as the carers in the family because of their economic position. This is linked to the idea of the cult of femininity. Describe this and get your depth of analysis by outlining the changes to this stereotypical representation by contrasting the strong characters Abercrombie identifies in many TV shows today. Secondly note how stereotypically women have been objectified by the media and connect these to Laura Mulvey's male gaze in your analysis. Suggest links to the subordination of women in society because of patriarchal ideology. In doing this you have linked together many concepts illustrating your knowledge, understanding and skills of analysis. Your ability to contrast ideas will score marks so the two factors can be a contrast; or add analysis in a separate paragraph, suggesting changes to the stereotypical portrayals of women that have taken place in recent years.

Question 2: Outline and explain **two** ways in which media representations of ethnic minorities can be seen as negative. **(10 marks) Spend 15 minutes on this response.**

HINTS TO HELP YOU RESPOND
Make two points of relevance that are distinct and detailed. Analyse by using the evidence of the diversity of media forms supplying endless choice or the pluralist understandings of the media reflecting the values of the society that exists at the moment. One point can be othering and the second point can be tokenism or coup-war-starvation syndrome. Connect concepts together to form a fuller picture of the processes of exclusion, stereotyping and labelling by the media. You can use concepts from other areas (the process of symbolic annihilation can link to the absence or condemnation that Stuart Hall analyses when identifying the portrayals of Black people as entertainers, slaves and natives). Link to Marxist ideas of power, values and norms for a deeper evaluation. The aggressive capitalism of the western world depends on promoting that lifestyle as a result of superior values.

Media: Media Representations of Age and Social Class

When evaluating the way the media represent age, the focus is on the old and the young. Both groups have been negatively stereotyped.

The Social Construction of Youth

Buckingham *et al* (2004) noted that **children** "have always been seen as a vulnerable audience in debates about broadcasting – an audience needing codes of practice and regulation". This vulnerability stems from children being easily influenced by the media.

The **social construction of youth** in terms of the binary opposites of **normality** and **abnormality** is a prevalent and enduring stereotype created by the news media. **Clockwork Orange Britain** (a reference to the novel by Anthony Burgess about a gang of teenagers who commit random acts of ultraviolence) is a headline from the *Daily Express* (2007) designed to trigger a news cycle of **moral panic**. Stories of violence, lawlessness and drug-taking are the focus of news about youth and there have been moral panics relating to knives, guns, ecstasy, raves and mods and rockers.

EVALUATION POINT

Coarse stereotypes surrounding Afro-Caribbean youth have created scapegoats, and problems in society are blamed on this group. Cohen (2002) argues this serves to bind people together in opposition to a folk devil or common enemy. From this a blanket labelling of youth as a problem develops. Geoffrey Parsons (1983) documented a similar labelling process in his book *Hooligan: A History of Respectable Fears*. The young are powerless and voiceless so their demonisation cannot be resisted by them.

The Young Consumers

Young people have been exploited as a growing affluent market for consumer goods. This trend is tracked to the 1950s. McChesney (2000) has identified MTV as a channel that sells a particular lifestyle to young people, with no significant changes between the advertisements aired on the network and the musical content. Everything that is broadcast is aimed at getting young people to buy goods.

EVALUATION POINT

The media's representation of youth is characterised by **ambivalence**; the media will briefly praise and then belligerently admonish young people. This can be linked to the formula of bad news equalling great news.

Representations of Youth

Representations of youth are linked to issues of class, ethnicity and gender by the media; the **Black mugger** highlighted in Stuart Hall's *Policing the Crisis: Mugging, the State, and Law and Order* (1978) is a classic example of this, in which Black youth is used as a symbol of the threat of violence. In the past girls have received less media attention than boys, who were seen as the main perpetrators of crime and antisocial behaviour. However, **ladette culture** has changed this. There is now less focus on one particular group.

Ageism

The old are presented as a **burden**, a social and economic problem, with the emphasis on poverty, ill health and the loss of independence. The old are portrayed as being out of touch with modern technology. Christopher Lasch (1979) argues (from a Marxist viewpoint) that this is because the old are economically of no further productive use to capitalism. Many do not work and have very little to spend. Old age should be feared and delayed. The emphasis on frailty is linked to the market in specialist medical products to help cope with ageing: drugs, surgery, technologies for greater mobility. All are profitable and skew the representation of the old.

Ageism is obvious in Hollywood, where female actors are considered unemployable once they pass the age of 35; their presence in films is regarded as decorative (they are sex objects).

Portrayals of the Working Class

Marxists see the media as controlled by the bourgeoisie. **Negative** portrayals of the working class serve the ruling-class ideology, exposing the poor as needing the assistance of the rich, their professionalism and skills guiding them and providing them with jobs. **Neo-Marxists** draw on the evidence of news broadcasts showing bias against trade unions which intensifies during strikes. The Glasgow University Media Group analysed the news media reporting of the 1984 miners' strike. Striking miners were reported as violent at every opportunity while police violence was rarely reported. Selection and editing of footage was biased and the bosses were given more opportunities to give their views, usually in an office where they could present themselves as calm, considerate and open to sensible negotiations. Miners, interviewed less frequently, were interviewed against the tumult of the picket line, with no time to prepare statements; they were perceived as the troublemakers embroiled in a pointless strike. Terms such as militant are attached to industrial action. These labels resonate in the public perception and what is wrong about the strike action; the news is socially constructed in favour of the elite.

Sympathetic Depictions of Working-Class Existence

Sympathetic depictions of working-class existence are found in the realism of Alan Bleasdale's *Boys from the Blackstuff* or Ken Loach's *I, Daniel Blake*; in the former the main character reacts to unemployment under Margaret Thatcher's 1980's government; in the latter the main character is subjected to austerity measures introduced by the Conservative governments in the 2010s.

Invisibility

Don Heider (2004) uses the term **invisibility** to explain how the poor are rarely reported as victims of crime. The middle classes are represented in a wider range of settings (in work, playing sport and music) but the working class are mainly associated with criminality. This **ghettoisation** produces restrictive stereotypes. The upper classes are portrayed as cultivated and with expertise from breeding and education. This is served by period dramas.

SUMMARY

- **Children are seen as vulnerable.**
- **Young people are socially constructed as a problem.**
- **The binary opposition of normal/abnormal is used to show the public abnormal youth.**
- **Moral panics result from the identification of abnormal behaviour that creates folk devils or scapegoats.**
- **The media have an ambivalent attitude to young people, they demonise them and pander to them as a market for consumer goods.**
- **Marxists believe that the old are shown as a burden because they no longer contribute to the production process.**
- **Ageism is reinforced by the absence of older characters from TV and movies. Roles are available for older men as wise figures.**
- **The news is socially constructed in favour of elite interests to portray the working classes and the unions in a negative way.**
- **Working-class stereotypes can be sympathetic but also mocking.**
- **The poor are invisible and ghettoised, and are not visible as victims of crime; the perpetrators of crimes are highly visible.**

QUICK TEST

1. What headline from a newspaper was taken from a novel by Anthony Burgess?

2. Which ethnic minority group are scapegoated by the media according to Cohen?

3. Which Marxist thinker believes that the old are represented as a burden because they are no longer part of the economic process?

4. Why do the media encourage the attitude that old age should be feared and delayed?

5. What sociologists' research has suggested that the elderly are rarely shown in the media and when they are they mainly provide comic relief?

6. Which theoretical view states that negative portrayals of the working class serves the ideology of the rich?

7. Which neo-Marxist group analysed the content of the news to find out about how trade unions were portrayed?

8. Which social class is stereotyped as buffoons?

9. Name the film that gives a sympathetic treatment to a benefit claimant subjected to Conservative austerity measures.

10. Who uses the term invisibility to explain how stories about crimes against the poor are not given any news coverage?

PRACTICE QUESTIONS

Question 1: Outline and explain two reasons why the representations of age may not be simple. (10 marks)
Spend 15 minutes on this response.

HINTS TO HELP YOU RESPOND

Give two clearly defined, explained and analysed points. Your first point should link to your knowledge of how the young are treated differently dependent on whether they are classed as children or youths. There is a lot of room for development of the ideas of vulnerability and protection from media itself, and also other harmful factors covered in the A Level course. These include the commercialisation of childhood. Your second point could be the portrayal of youth as normal and abnormal. Unpack the concept of binary oppositions. Include concepts that support the portrayal of youth as abnormal (for example, deviancy amplification stemming from moral panics and the demonising of the youth as folk devils). If all these points are explained correctly you will score full marks. Your analysis can be taken from the idea that youth are seen as a lucrative market and source of profit by companies. As such they cannot be portrayed as too demonic, except when youth rebellion is being transformed into money. This has happened with other youth culture (punk, hip hop, rap).

ITEM A

Many believe that the working classes are restricted to a few stereotypical representations in the media, while the middle and upper classes are represented by a wider cast of characters. The middle classes and the higher classes are often portrayed as leaders, successes, artists or innovators.

Programmes like *Benefits Britain* replicate the same narrow view of the working classes, while the royal family is seen on TV carrying out charitable work or opening civic buildings.

Question 2: Applying material from **Item A** and your knowledge, evaluate the view that the media rarely represents the interests of the working classes in society. **(20 marks) Spend 30 minutes on this response.**

HINTS TO HELP YOU RESPOND

Start by tackling the question head on. Try to think of a summary sentence to answer the question. This will set the tone of your thinking on this topic. For example: It has long been the criticism of both Marxists and neo-Marxists that the media portrayals of the working classes undermine social class solidarity and support the power elite in their dominance. The power elite own the huge corporations that produce the media messages that show themselves in a favourable light. It could be said that with ever increasing concentration of media ownership, the distorted representations of the workers has become worse.

You have to establish a connection to the question and Item A and a key theoretical view. Also link to other aspects of the course. Behind any question you are given there will be links for you to draw on. Here the link is to the ownership and control part of the course. Once you have established this point you need to evidence it and explain it through the use of concepts that have been examined. These include invisibility, ghettoisation, and the use of binary opposites to discredit, devalue or negatively label workers. Evaluate using pluralist theories of choice, diversity of media showing a wide range of information. Your conclusion should directly answer the question but sustain the reasoning of your essay.

Media: Media Representations of Sexuality and Disability

Homosexuality

Sexuality, a person's sexual behaviour or characteristics, is seen as normal by the media if they are heterosexual. The media sexualises men just as women have been sexually objectified.

The media has **distorted** the image of gay people by associating homosexuality with **deviancy**. Lisa Bennett (2000) analysed 50 years of media coverage of homosexuals and found that they were linked to criminality without evidence. This led to the image of homosexuals as being inferior to heterosexuals. An example of negative prejudice are the headlines published by a national newspaper in the 1980s calling AIDS "the gay plague". This hostility was replicated in 1998 when a headline asked: "Are we being run by a Gay Mafia?"

EVALUATION POINT

Craig (1992) contends that homosexual characters are rarely portrayed and when they are, these characters are stereotypes; the audience may be amused by that stereotype or interested in the negative psychological portrayal.

Camp Depictions of Gay Men

Camp depictions of gay men are intended to make visible to an audience what is otherwise invisible. Dyer (2002) suggests that gay people are subject to symbolic annihilation. The camp, effeminate, colourful depictions of gay men are deemed as a safe way to indicate to the audience what is actually unknowable: a character's sexuality. There are suggestions that camp characters are able to act in ways that are **subversive** to authority figures, but Dyer believes this safe stereotype is less challenging to heterosexual notions of masculinity.

EVALUATION POINT

When examining medieval carnivals Bakhtin (1941) saw that the social order was inverted for a short time; the dominant ideology was challenged and authority was ridiculed. Camp personalities like Kenneth Williams and Julian Clary perform a similar function to what Dyer has indicated.

Depictions of Gay Characters

A more diverse range of gay characters has been depicted in recent years. Russell Davies created the TV series *Queer as Folk,* which was both attacked and lauded by many viewers and critics. Russell Davies is gay and he created characters that did not rely on their (homo)sexuality as the sole reference for audience identification.

EVALUATION POINT

Gross (1993) finds that the **heterosexual gaze** constructs representations of homosexuals. This makes for characters that are flamboyant or stereotyped because heterosexual men who create the characters cannot write about "just plain gay folks".

Depictions of Lesbians

The media's depictions of lesbians has run a similar course although in the past lesbian characters were even less visible, and appeared as **butch stereotypes**. This has been changed by the **pink pound**. There is an economic advantage that can be gained by creating products for the gay community (films and dramas). Gay culture has had a growing impact on heterosexual culture.

Representations of People with Disabilities

Representations of people with **disabilities** in the media centre on the **disability itself**; characters with disabilities are made interesting because they lack something. Jenny Morris (1997) makes a compelling argument for the explanation of the numbers of characters with disabilities that do appear being mostly men. Her focus is on portrayals of dependency and of lack. She argues that "women do not have to be portrayed with disabilities in order to present an image of vulnerability and dependency".

Stereotyping of People with Disabilities

Another standard depiction of people with disabilities was through the binary opposition of **normality and abnormality**. The growth in programmes featuring people with disabilities and disability issues has declined. Paul Darke (2003) argued that this is due to greater competition for advertising revenue and the need to secure larger audiences in the media marketplace. Even though there are more channels, the competition between channels has intensified and minority interest programming has been forced out.

The **gaze** is a useful concept for understanding the stereotyping of people with disabilities in the media. Disabled representations frequently fall into the category of **objects of curiosity**. This continues to be true. Barnes (1992) came up with these stereotypes that fit the full scope of representations of people with disabilities: pitiable and pathetic; object of violence; sinister and evil; curiosities; super-cripples (depicted as their own worst enemy); dependent (a burden); sexually abnormal; incapable; ordinary or normal.

Telethons

Telethons have been a source of analysis by sociologists. The image of people with disabilities as dependent is reinforced by telethons. Karpf (1988) argues that the entertainment and relief from guilt that the public finds in telethons is a distraction from the real problems that people with disabilities face. The environment disempowers people with disabilities but governments will not take action to solve these problems while the focus remains on lack of mobility rather than planning.

Mental Disabilities

Philo (1999), carrying out research for the Glasgow University Media Group, uncovered evidence that the news media reported on people with mental disabilities in such a way to make the public afraid of people with mental disabilities. This fear stemmed from the focus in the media on violence and mental illness.

The media is a powerful force in shaping negative, isolating stereotypes of disability.

SUMMARY

- Sexuality is not apparent to the viewer and therefore distortions of the characteristics of homosexual characters have been created to help identify gay characters to audiences.

- Audiences are invited to be amused by the stereotypes of gay men.

- Camp depictions are both subversive and harmful stereotypes.

- Stereotypes are constructed through the heterosexual gaze.

- Disability as deviance; these representations reassure the able-bodied of their difference.

- Normality and abnormality; a binary opposition which again reassures the able-bodied by being denoted normal in contrast to the abnormal disabled stereotype.

- The able-bodied gaze constructs people with disabilities as objects of curiosity.

- The Glasgow University Media Group found the depictions of people with mental disabilities to be very powerful in shaping negative stereotypes.

QUICK TEST

1. Which sociologist analysed 50 years of media coverage of homosexuals, finding that they were linked to criminality without evidence?

2. Which stereotype of gay men is thought to be both subversive and a safe stereotype, reassuring to heterosexual ideas about masculinity?

3. Who wrote that the heterosexual gaze is responsible for the flamboyant stereotypes of gay men in the media?

4. What phrase sums up the spending power of the gay community?

5. What binary opposition is employed in the depiction of disability by the media?

6. What is Paul Darke's explanation for the fall in minority programming for people with disabilities in recent years?

7. How does the able-bodied gaze represent people with disabilities?

8. How many viewers with disabilities did Ross interview?

9. State two ways in which telethons benefit the public?

10. Who found evidence of the harmful depiction of stereotypes of people with mental disabilities by the media?

PRACTICE QUESTIONS

Question 1: Outline and explain **two** reasons why the way in which the media portray disability is thought to be harmful. **(10 marks) Spend 15 minutes on this response.**

HINTS TO HELP YOU RESPOND
Provide two clear paragraphs of detailed explanation with clear explanations of any concepts that you use. Remember to link your answer directly to the question. Your first reason could be that disability is shown as deviance. This is harmful as it creates a stereotype of people with disabilities that leads to their exclusion. Explain how this happens. Link in the concepts of normal and abnormal and how the binary opposition is employed to reinforce the negative labels, shoring up the manufactured identity of deviant or abnormal. Analyse this concept with the ideas of diversity and the growth of representations of people with disabilities, then the recent decline as market forces conspire to exclude people with disabilities from the media. Secondly, you may include Philo's evidence from the research he carried out into the portrayal of mental disability. To give this depth, support it with concepts from the chapter on 'Media: Ideological Factors Affecting the Social Construction of the News' in which the social construction of the news is examined or where media effects are explored in depth in the chapter on 'Media: Media Effects' to show the impact of the media can be powerful.

ITEM A
The media has come to terms with the fact that homosexuality can be presented without resorting to the stereotypes of camp or butch. This was once the only way of allowing the visibility of gay characters, by heterosexual writers creating subversive camp characters. Today the pink economy is too valuable not to include a range of homosexual characters in the media.

Question 2: Using material from **Item A**, analyse two reasons for the under-representation of homosexuals in the media becoming less problematic. **(10 marks) Spend 15 minutes on this response.**

HINTS TO HELP YOU RESPOND
Linking to Item A, explain the reasons for camp depictions of gay men in the media. This will cover the threat to the masculinity of the male heterosexual audience. The analysis of the notion of carnival and the camp character as a voice of subversion of societal norms can be explored. Be sure to evaluate the positions of gay men in the media, are plain gay folks represented now? Your second point can be around the commercial viability of depicting homosexuals. The pink economy is the same point as the pink pound. Bring in Klein to add depth to your answer and develop your analysis through the more general adoption of gay culture into mainstream culture.

Media: Media Effects

The Impact of the Media on the Audience

The impact that the media has on the audience has been simplified to a **cause and effect relationship** by **the hypodermic syringe/needle model**. The media are strong and the audience are weak. The media message is directly injected into the veins of the passive audience. This is often thought of as an unsatisfactory explanation of the media's effect as it treats the audience as unthinking robots that accept the media messages uncritically, without resistance. The impact is immediate. The audience act on the message; if the message is violent then the audience become violent (**copycat violence**). Ideological messages are transmitted that cannot be resisted; the message is like a drug, altering thoughts.

EVALUATION POINT

Evidence for these immediate effects is not widely found. The audience is treated as a gullible, homogeneous mass. There is evidence the audience are heterogeneous and active. The media's power is seen as greater than individual experience or primary socialisation – the family, or other secondary sources such as education. Rather than desensitising an audience the violence may sensitise viewers, making the viewer empathise with the victims of violence. Violence can be cathartic, enabling viewers to vent anger while watching it. This can be true in gaming. Fesbach and Sanger (1971) found that of two groups given non-violent and violent materials to view, the former were more aggressive after a six-week period of exposure. Violent media acted like a safety valve giving cathartic release to bottled-up emotions.

The Two-Step Flow Model

Katz and Lazarsfeld (1955) addressed the flaws of the hypodermic syringe model. The other experiences of audiences, the influence of their family, their own beliefs, their peers, school or workplace will all have an influence on reactions. This is known as **the two-step flow model**.

Step one is the media messages reaching the audience. In **Step two** the audience discuss the messages of the media where the opinion leader is influential. The opinion leader's views are selectively passed on to affect a group, this group can in turn influence others.

EVALUATION POINT

The model does not explain how the audience is divided into opinion leaders and their group. It fails to explain how some audience members become active while the majority remain passive. Even the opinion leaders must be influenced by the media message initially, and there is a case for arguing that the media are shaped by the audience. There is room for manipulation of the group by the opinion leader but this relationship is not explained fully. The active interpretations of the media between groups is not a point that is explored, as members of different groups socialise, interpret and redefine messages.

The Heterogeneous Audience

The two-step-flow model does take account of the audience being heterogeneous (varied) and active. The opinion leader is selecting or filtering information from the source of media messages. The social dynamism or web of relations within which messages from the media are discussed is recognised. Messages are not just received and processed in isolation.

EVALUATION POINT

Morley's (1980) study of *Nationwide* viewers' reactions to news showed that they reacted in three ways, just as Hall had outlined in *Encoding/decoding* (1980). The message was either not challenged (dominant), was partially but not wholly accepted (negotiated), or there was outright rejection of the message (oppositional) by the viewer/reader.

The Cultural Effects Model

A very influential active audience model is called **the cultural effects model**. It can be likened to a dripping tap because the influence of the media is seen over a long time as shaping our common-sense views of the world. The ideas of a powerful elite are seen as the norm because the dominant ideologies shape our experiences over a long time. An example would be the idea that men are the breadwinners and problem-solvers is presented to us from birth and we succumb to this dominant way of thinking. Personal experience can then alter this common-sense or hegemonic (dominant) view of the world (for example through direct experience of strike action).

EVALUATION POINT

Criticism of this view would be that not all journalists are creating content that supports the value consensus. Media content explores the many ways in which power is concentrated and unjustly exercised. Philo of the GUMG researched audience reactions to the miners' strike and found that the media were often so powerful in their messages that the hypodermic syringe model worked as an explanation. However, there were variances, and audiences did change their views depending on personal experience, supporting an active audience model like the cultural effects theory.

Uses and Gratifications Model

The advantages of the cultural effects model are that it shows the audience as active but influenced by prolonged media exposure to dominant ideologies. This then shows how media bias can operate in our world of heterogeneous audiences that are far from passive.

The **uses and gratifications model** favoured by Blumler and McQuail (1968) recognises the audience's ability to satisfy a wide range of needs. The needs vary because audiences are heterogeneous. This means that the television can be wallpaper, a background to other activities. Media can confirm identity and personal values, it can explore our own interest in personal relationships, and simply provide us with entertainment.

EVALUATION POINT

The uses and gratification model is seen as ignoring the influence of group dynamics or the social context, placing too much power in the hands of the individual to shape their own viewing habits when advertisers and programme-makers provide a selection from which we then choose. Thus the model ignores the power of the elite to shape tastes to sell products to the audience.

The Impact of Violent Media

Mass killings and violence have often been linked to violent films or violent video games. These negative effects have been said to desensitise audiences or normalise violence. Cumberbatch (2004) conducted a review of 3,500 studies on the effects of violent media and found no evidence for causal links; violent media does not make people violent. Young (1981) found positive impacts of violent media. Audience learning of the consequences of violent action sensitised them to violence. The context in which violence takes place has been ignored argues Morrison (1999). In certain situations the violence is for comedic impact. Research has often been carried out in **laboratory experiments** but this gives rise to misleading results. The copycat violence proven by Bandura, Ross and Ross (1961) in which children imitated a woman attacking a doll and then an adult dressed as a clown has been criticised because of the artificiality of the laboratory setting. People know they are being observed and the Hawthorne effect is unavoidable (changing your behaviour because you know you are being observed). Laboratory experiments are usually short-term studies and so do not look at the long-term effects of exposure to violence.

EVALUATION POINT

The media make violence seem worse than it is and arrests may increase as people become more aware of a group or problem. This is known as **deviancy amplification**. Cohen (1972) found that the media create folk devils of young people and create moral panics around issues such as theft, knife-carrying, drug-taking and raves. This scapegoating of people can serve the purpose of distracting them from economic crises. People believe that violent crime is more prevalent than it actually is because of the focus on violence in news-reporting. Some sociologists argue that we have socially constructed all violence as negative. Sport can be violent but it is not harmful to society.

SUMMARY

- The hypodermic syringe model states the media has immediate and direct effects on a passive audience.

- This model is used to explain copycat violence.

- Violent media can act as a safety valve, releasing trapped emotions and is cathartic.

- The two-step flow model takes account of other influences and group interactions when interpreting the media message. An opinion leader (step one) is influenced by the media and passes their ideas through a group of people (step two).

- The cultural effects model is like a dripping tap shaping our common sense view of the world over a long period of time.

- Not all journalists create content that is in agreement with the dominant ideology.

- The uses and gratifications model explains how the audiences make conscious choices in actively deciding which one of four needs must be met (entertainment, personal relationships, personal identity and wallpaper).

- Laboratory style experiments to prove links between the media and violence in real life are flawed. Violence can sensitise people, audiences are heterogeneous and influenced by other factors.

QUICK TEST

1. In the hypodermic syringe model of the media are the audience weak or strong?

2. What particular type of violence is thought to be generated in the audience because of the hypodermic syringe model?

3. What is another term for violent media being seen as a safety valve for bottled-up emotions?

4. Who came up with the two-step flow model?

5. According to Hall and Morley, in which three ways can media messages be received or interpreted?

6. In what four ways does the media satisfy the audiences' personal choices or needs according to Blumler and McQuail?

7. How many studies did Cumberbatch review to be able to dismiss the link between viewing violent media content and committing violent actions?

8. Whose famous study showed children a film of a woman beating up a doll and then a real clown and recorded the children's reactions to this?

9. What is the Hawthorne effect?

10. What is deviancy amplification?

PRACTICE QUESTIONS

Question 1: Outline and explain **two** ways in which the media can influence the audience. **(10 marks) Spend 15 minutes on this response.**

HINTS TO HELP YOU RESPOND

The question assumes that the media influences the audience. This is the effects approach. You can choose to generalise about effects models or be specific in exploring particular models or concepts. Your first way would be to evaluate the hypodermic syringe model. This model has shown that the audience are weak and the media influence strong. Cite examples of this analysis from the Bandura, Ross and Ross study of copycat violence. Analysis will focus on the ideas of Fesbach and Sanger and the cathartic influence of violent media content. Your second point can be an analysis of the neo-Marxist cultural effects model with an explanation of the gradual influence of the media to shape ideology to the dominant or elite ideas. Analyse this with a look at the uses and gratifications model.

ITEM A

In 1938 a radio broadcast of HG Wells's book *The War of the Worlds* narrating a Martian invasion of Earth created panic in the USA. The panic was caused because some listeners believed the broadcast to be a live factual broadcast. Those people that missed the beginning of the broadcast had not realised this was a dramatisation. Those who were more isolated were more likely to take the broadcast as factual reporting. This has been used as evidence of both the hypodermic model and the cultural effects model.

Question 2: Applying material from **Item A** and your knowledge, evaluate the usefulness of the cultural effects model of the media. **(20 marks) Spend around 30 minutes on this response.**

HINTS TO HELP YOU RESPOND

These essay questions are best answered with a detailed explanation of the concept or theory or model that is the focus of the question. This then must be evaluated by looking at the strengths and weaknesses of the model. This will include comparing the cultural effects model to other models. In comparing the cultural effects model to the hypodermic syringe model we can see that it is an improvement because it takes account of the different types of audience, the active nature rather than passive nature of the audience. Of course the item is evidence of the cultural effects model because not all individuals reacted the same and so social context is perhaps taken account of more by the cultural effects model. This may also allow you to list the many limitations of the hypodermic syringe model. To bring your essay back to the question, be sure to cite the evidence of Philo and the GUMG – some audiences were directly influenced by media content; however, if not all members are influenced to the same extent then the hypodermic syringe model has to be inadequate. Explore the work of Hall and the different positions of dominant, negotiated and oppositional audience members. Your final point can be to contrast the cultural effects model with the uses and gratifications model, which gives the audience greater power in the relationship of audience and media. Your conclusion should support either your feeling that the cultural effects model is an improvement on the hypodermic syringe model but perhaps stops short of seeing the consumer of media as completely powerful and autonomous.

Item A

Traditional Marxism is concerned with the class divide in society between the bourgeoisie and proletariat. Traditional Marxists see crime as a reaction by the working class to their exploited position in society; they also note that ruling-class crime occurs as the capitalist system encourages unscrupulous competition in which criminal activity has become embedded.

Neo-Marxists agree with traditional Marxism in considering society to be based on a significant level of inequality; they, however, see crime as an active choice by the individual.

Question 1: Applying material from Item A and your knowledge, evaluate the Marxist perspective of crime and deviance. (30 marks)

Top Mark Response:

Marxism focuses on the inequality in capitalist society, as stated in Item A, "Traditional Marxists see crime as a reaction by the working class to their position in society". Marxists suggest that capitalism is criminogenic, causing crime in all social classes. In society the proletariat (working class) are forced to wage-slave for the bourgeoisie (ruling, or capitalist class) as they own nothing but their ability to work. The bourgeoisie own the means of production in society, this ranges from factories to businesses. The bourgeoisie are fewer in society, though they hold the overall wealth.

> The response starts with a clear explanation of Marxist views of society, referencing the item. This shows an understanding of the perspective in question.

This inequality can cause the proletariat to take to crime out of necessity in order to survive through the poverty that their lower-ranked place in society inflicts on them. This Marxist view is useful in explaining utilitarian crimes that benefit the working class. Marxists see the bourgeoisie as controlling the media and, in turn, benefitting from capitalist advertising of material goods. These adverts may create a sense of relative deprivation within the working class as they

see themselves not being able to afford the glittering prizes afforded by the bourgeoisie. Supporting this view, left realists see relative deprivation as leading to marginalisation, exclusion from society, which further causes working-class crime and the development of subcultures in which crime is accepted. Unlike Marxists they do not see capitalism as the sole source of this.

> The Marxist view of crime in all classes is explained (see example below for ruling-class crime) and also the respondent has evaluated the concept of relative deprivation with views of left realism. This shows an ability to draw upon synoptic links with other theories for support.

Marxists also note the impact of capitalism on crimes of the ruling class. Item A mentions the "unscrupulous competition" that corporations face; this can lead to legal boundaries being crossed in order to make better profits. Tombs and Whyte argue that corporations are constructed through law and politics in ways that impel them to cause harm to people and the environment. They suggest that the capitalist system causes corporate crime to be deeply rooted in the practices of many businesses. This Marxist theory is useful as it explains that crime is not just a working-class phenomenon as official statistics may suggest, it also occurs in the ruling class.

> A good use of theorists in Tombs and Whyte shows that the respondent is able to show knowledge and understanding of the Marxist perspective. The response could include official statistics that show working-class patterns of crime. It could also offer a Marxist critique of the usefulness of official statistics on crime.

This Marxist explanation of corporate crime in order to compete in a capitalist system fails to explain non-utilitarian white collar crimes. For example, the GP Harold Shipman was believed to have murdered over 200 of his patients over 23 years in practice, with no aims of financial gain. This cannot be explained in terms of wealth inequality, or a frustration about status in society and therefore causes problems for Marxist explanations of crime.

Marxists argue that the working class are kept in a state of false class consciousness in which their exploitation is legitimised. This is a means of reducing their awareness of exploitation and maintaining the dominant position of the bourgeoisie.

Neo-Marxists suggest that the traditional Marxist view of crime is too deterministic, they note that working-class crime does not simply take place in order to gain material possessions that are unobtainable in a world of relative deprivation. They see crime as voluntaristic, an act of choice. Taylor, Walton and Young argue that criminals are not acting passively, they are actively trying to change society for the better.

Taylor *et al* believe that in order to create a full social theory of deviance we must look at the structural causes of a crime (as traditional Marxism would), and also at the meaning of the crime for the individual committing it (as a social action theorist would). They see many working-class crimes as actions to take from the rich and redistribute wealth to the poor.

Taylor, Walton and Young have been heavily criticised as romanticising working-class crime as almost a Robin Hood-like act. Neo-Marxism fails to acknowledge intra-class crime that happens in working-class areas, committed by members of the working class against other working-class individuals.

Functionalists argue against Marxist views that crime is the result of working-class exploitation in society, they see crime as an integral and healthy part of all societies. Rather than the neo-Marxist view that crime is an active choice often aimed at redistributing wealth in society, functionalists see crime as occurring when the value consensus is weakened and anomie takes hold, with individuals becoming confused about their role in society. This is a sign of egoism in individuals according to functionalists, as opposed to

the neo-Marxist view that crime is in the interest of the whole of society.

Feminist thinkers suggest that Marxists focus too heavily on the class inequality in society as a cause of crime, they suggest that patriarchy and the subordination of women is the main form of inequality in society. This inequality causes crime, not only out of frustration as women become liberated in society (according to liberal feminists) but also as a result of deals within the class system that fail for women. Pat Carlen notes that female crime occurs when women are denied a class or gender deal in society. Marxist feminists see capitalist society viewing women as a cheap exploitable form of labour. This view supports Marxist concepts of crime as it sees capitalism as the cause of female crime; however, radical feminists see inequality caused by patriarchy as much more concerning than the inequality caused by social class.

Postmodernism criticises the Marxist view of crime as being outdated. Postmodernists see Marxism as a meta-narrative, simply being one view of the truth of society. They see society as too fragmented and diverse to view structures such as class being the main cause of crime in society. They also note that crime can be an active choice as opposed to simply a response to capitalism.

In conclusion, Marxist views of crime rely heavily on the concept that class exploitation exists so strongly in society that crime is a rational response to inequality, others see this as too deterministic.

Question 2: Outline two advantages of labelling theory in order to understand crime and deviance. (4 marks)

Top Mark Response:

- Labelling theory takes a micro-approach to society, looking in-depth at individuals and their impact on others around them. This detailed approach is effective in analysing exactly how crime and deviance are socially constructed.

- Labelling theory allows a person to see the impact of society's reactions to a person's behaviour on their future acts. It allows us to question the impact of labels on the act of secondary deviance.

> Here the respondent has kept the points to two separate bullet points, ensuring that there is a real clarity between each point made. The response is fairly short but precise as the respondent has kept a close watch over the time taken to respond.

Question 3: Outline three reasons why statistics show female crime to occur less than male crime in society. (6 marks)

Top Mark Response:

- Chivalry thesis suggests that females do commit more crimes, possibly as many as males, the statistics may lack representativeness as men in the criminal justice system are reluctant to criminalise women.
- Heidensohn suggests that females have less opportunity to commit crime in society than males as they experience patriarchal control at home, at work and in public.
- Messerschmidt sees males as needing to accomplish masculinity, many males are denied this opportunity and see criminal ways of showing masculinity due to their subordinated masculinities.

> Three short points made, each starting on a separate line. Here the respondent uses theorists to show that they have a clear knowledge of the origins of the points.

Question 4: Outline and explain two ways in which the media can be censored or regulated. (10 marks)

Top Mark Response:

Censorship refers to the regulation of speech, communication or other information that may be considered objectionable, harmful or sensitive by a certain group. In the media, censorship may come from the government, by an independent media company or through self-regulation.

> The response starts with a clear definition and understanding of the term.

One such example is a public service such as the BBC who are subject to certain legal guidelines and restrictions. The BBC aims to be independent, impartial and honest at all times and, unlike some other news companies, does not have a left- or right-leaning political bias. The BBC gains funding from the public but also from the government and in order to secure this they must stick to the regulations in its charter. One example of this can be seen by the watershed; this is regulation that states that nudity, sex, violence and foul language is censored before 9pm. After 9pm these things may be shown so long as a warning is given prior to the programme starting. However, many believe that impartiality is rarely achieved.

> The response describes an example really clearly and also uses an example to back it up in the form of the BBC; key words such as bias and charter are also used.

An example of self-regulation can be seen in the British press, which is classed as a free press; this means that newspapers are allowed to argue from a political stance and viewpoint with no obligation to be impartial or unbiased. The regulation comes in the form of the Press Complaints Commission (PCC) who monitor standards; therefore if a newspaper prints an untrue or inaccurate story then they must issue an apology and amend the incorrect original statement; however, this is often criticised as the amendment can be very small in comparison to the original story. One such example is an inaccurate description about the sexuality of a celebrity that is later retracted.

> Again, the second point uses a clear example by referring to the PCC; this shows good knowledge and understanding to gain marks.

Question 5: Applying material from Item B, analyse two examples of media effects models other than those mentioned in the item. (10 marks)

Top Mark Response:

A model that shares some characteristics with the hypodermic syringe model as referred to in Item B is the two-step flow model. This normative model was first introduced by Katz and Lazerfield and suggests that media is delivered to its audience through some filtering. Media is delivered to the major outlets such as TV channels and newspapers; they then decide if it is newsworthy, then shape it and deliver this news in the manner they wish to. The public then receive the message and pass it on to their friends and family; however, this is often edited, exaggerated or embellished. The similarity with the hypodermic model is that people often passively believe what they are being to because they trust the source. However, this is often criticised as being a rather outdated view of an audience response as a variety of responses are available to individuals in late modern society.

> The first point uses a model, a key sociologist and then uses counterarguments to gain AO2 and AO3 marks.

A model that suggests the audience take a far more active role is the uses and gratifications model, which argues that consumers actually pick and choose their own media and messages to fulfil their own particular uses and needs. McQuail notes that a person may follow media for different reasons at different times such as factual news for research, identify shaping through Facebook, solidarity through online gaming, or reality television for entertainment and escapism.

This model suggests the advent of new media and its saturation and variety means that users have far more choice and can pick up and put down media at their own discretion. However, this model ignores that media saturation often means that we do not have the ability to avoid a daily barrage of media, which may mean that individuals are still heavily influenced by media they do not select.

> The second point follows the pattern of the first by using a model, a key sociologist and then uses counterarguments to gain AO2 and AO3 marks.

Question 6: Applying material from Item C and your knowledge, evaluate the view that "Religion continues to be a patriarchal institution". (20 marks)

Top Mark Response:

The term patriarchy means male domination and theorists from all different factions of feminism have long argued that religion is a patriarchal institution that often legitimises the unequal power balance between males and females. However, other theorists believe that feminists are ignoring the changing attitudes of religion, particularly in recent times.

> The introduction clearly defines what patriarchy is, introduces feminism and sets up the two sides of the debate.

Daly states that religions are male-dominated, hierarchical institutions that simply serve the interests of a sexist society; focusing on Islam and Christianity in particular, Daly notes how women are rarely found in positions of power and influence, from God(s) and the prophets to the figureheads in places of worship. There is plenty of evidence to show that women are excluded from power in religious organisations.

De Beauvoir takes a more Marxist feminist approach to religion by saying that religion justifies female suffering on earth by promising them they will receive equality in heaven; this theory shows a parallel with Marx's theory on how the proletariat put up with their lowly status because of the promise of a better afterlife. For De Beauvoir religion maintains and justifies women staying at home to support the man and is the reason why patriarchy remains. However, many Marxists dispute this and say that capitalism is the driving force of inequality, not patriarchy.

> This passage shows good knowledge, use of sociologists, but also some criticism and counter-arguments.

Holm suggests that religion maintains patriarchy by enforcing the views through biology and sexuality. In terms of biology, religious texts often discuss the female role as the mother and caregiver as natural and important, this therefore traps the female into submitting to traditional roles by transmitting the message that this is her purpose in life.

The sexuality argument is developed by radical feminists who believe that females are either portrayed as virginal and pure or as temptresses and sexual distractions from worship, the classic Christian example being Eve and the temptation of Adam with the apple. As mentioned in Item C, many radical feminists feel it is the female who is punished by having to cover up in the Islamic faith when it is actually the man carrying out the sin of lustful desire. Likewise, in many Jewish synagogues the females sit behind the men so that they are not distracted by the female congregation. Of course, this view is often contested as being a choice rather than being forced, suggesting that individuals have the free will to interpret and adapt religious practices for themselves.

> This response both uses and builds on the item as a good response should do for a 20-mark question, there is continuous use of sociologists and key terms throughout the essay.

El-Saadawi looks at even more extreme examples of patriarchal attitudes to women in religion such as female genital mutilation, something that she suffered herself as a child. She has campaigned hard for the practice to stop but fears there has been a recent relapse in line with the rise of some fundamental religions. El-Saadawi has long been a campaigner against religion, which she sees as a key institution in maintaining and promoting patriarchy.

Therefore, for feminists there are clear elements of sexism in all faiths, even direct passages from religious texts such as the Quran state about the power and value of a woman being worth less than that of a man. However, despite these views, statistics show that females are actually more likely to belong to a faith and be part of a mainstream religion than men.

This could possibly be due to early primary socialisation when females are taught to be passive or conformist; therefore, this relates to more traditional or conservative characteristics of mainstream religion. Another suggestion is that because females are the primary caregivers, going to church and raising children to be religious is an extension of their expected role in society. Indeed, Davie notes that many females view God as a form of love rather than control. In contrast to this, many new religious movements offer women the chance to challenge patriarchy and promote social change.

The new right perspective criticises the feminist viewpoint for ignoring how biology dictates roles, for example that females are depicted in religious texts as the caregiver and provider because they are the ones that have children. Therefore, religion simply confirms the natural order of gender roles.

Defenders of the Islamic faith also note that issues such as female veiling, the hijab or wearing of the burka can have positive functions for the female as it can protect them from sexual harassment by men and also affirm their Muslim identity. Woodhead argues that many females actually see the traditional dress as empowering rather than oppressive and often it is their own personal choice to wear it rather than enforced.

This essay benefits from analysing a range of different feminisms and also different religions; responses tend to focus on Christianity but also look at Islam and Hinduism, too, in order to gain more knowledge marks.

Woodhead continues her discussion by stating that not all religion is patriarchal; for example, Hinduism and other polytheistic religions in which goddesses have a high status; she also notes that since 1992 the Church of England has allowed females into the priesthood and around 20 per cent of priests are females, therefore attitudes are becoming more relaxed and changing in some factions of religion.

In conclusion, then, there seems to be a contradiction between many feminist arguments on religion and what the statistics are telling us. Feminists suggest that religion remains patriarchal but it is obviously an attractive proposition, offering a sense of community and solace to many females as they are more likely to attend a place of worship and practise their faith than men are; indeed, this is backed up by records that show us that although secularisation is occurring in many places, it is men that are more likely to turn their backs on religion than women.

There is strong knowledge throughout this response and a range of A02 and A03 points, too, through the use of analysis and evaluation. Each paragraph looks at another aspect of feminism and there are a variety of theorists used throughout the essay.

Quick Test Answers

DAY 1

Beliefs in Society: Perspectives on Religion
QUICK TEST (Page 6)
1. Consensus sees religion as bringing people together; conflict sees religion as dividing people.
2. When objects have religious significance or symbolism.
3. Althusser.
4. Hegemony.
5. Protestantism.
6. That it keeps and maintains traditions.
7. That females are pushed to the edges or not accepted by religion.
8. Bauman.
9. The decrease in the popularity and importance of religion.
10. The objects and their shared meanings bring people together.

Beliefs in Society: Religion's Impact on Changes in Society
QUICK TEST (Page 10)
1. That religion can cause a political or social development.
2. The idea that a certain number of people have been selected for heaven by God.
3. Living a pure and moral life.
4. Martin Luther King.
5. Latin America.
6. 1960s.
7. Catholicism.
8. Movements which focus on poverty and the saving of people due to belief in the second coming of Christ.
9. Worsley.
10. Functionalists, Marxists and feminists.

Beliefs in Society: The Secularisation Debate
QUICK TEST (Page 14)
1. Practice, thinking and institutions.
2. People actively seek out more rational explanations for events, beyond events simply being the act of a supernatural power.
3. That logical thinking and science replace myth and magic.
4. Evidence that is observable or measurable.
5. The Christian belief in Adam and Eve or the Muslim belief in the prophet Mohammed would be such examples.
6. The belief in two or more religions or an acceptance of more than one religious practice.
7. It means the loss of the sacred.
8. Postmodernism.
9. The belief that God cannot be proven or disproven.
10. Most commonly in Europe although China also has a high percentage of atheists.

Beliefs in Society: New Forms of Religion and the Position of Religion Today
QUICK TEST (Page 18)
1. Selected beliefs/practices from a range of religions.
2. Abandoning or leaving a religion.
3. Choosing different practices from different faiths.
4. Any two from crystal healing, meditation, yoga, horoscopes or astral projection.
5. No expectancy to have to attend or follow; they are individualised practices.
6. That faiths often lose popularity but then have a revival.
7. Religions that come back into the interest of the public.
8. That our lives are dominated by media all the time.
9. Hadden and Shupe.
10. Norris and Inglehart.

Beliefs in Society: Religion and Globalisation
QUICK TEST (Page 22)
1. Throughout northern Europe.
2. A person who does not believe there is enough evidence to believe in God.
3. That religion works in the interest of male domination.
4. Castells.
5. Firmly believing in a faith without any wavering.

6. Any two from Judaism, Christianity or Islam.
7. Bruce.
8. Outdated.
9. An Islamic militant fighting for the holy war.
10. Beck.

DAY 2

Beliefs in Society: Types of Religious Organisation
QUICK TEST (Page 26)
1. Churches, denominations, sects and cults.
2. Troeltsch.
3. To be excluded from religion or excluded from society as a whole.
4. The belief that a particular faith holds the true messages and ideas.
5. Denominations.
6. Cult (or denomination).
7. World-rejecting.
8. The personal search for truth rather than listening to the word of a religious leader.
9. When a person becomes dissatisfied with religious explanations.
10. Bruce.

Beliefs in Society: Religious Ideology and Scientific Thinking
QUICK TEST (Page 30)
1. Study without bias.
2. Evidence that can be measured or observed.
3. Positivists.
4. Beginning with a hypothesis and drawing a conclusion.
5. The attempt to prove theories wrong.
6. Popper.
7. That science works within limitations/restrictions.
8. A pattern or model that science often works within.
9. Polvani.
10. Ideological and utopian.

Crime and Deviance: Functionalist Theories, Subcultural and Strain Theories
QUICK TEST (Page 34)
1. Socialisation.
2. Structural factors and cultural factors.
3. Crime that is for the goal of financial success.
4. Groups fall back on drugs or alcohol.
5. Anomie.
6. Innovation.
7. Status frustration.
8. Conflict subcultures.
9. Rosenfeld and Messner.
10. Those who conform to the value consensus.

Crime and Deviance: Labelling Theory
QUICK TEST (Page 38)
1. Howard Becker.
2. Their common-sense knowledge.
3. Moral entrepreneurs.
4. Mods and rockers.
5. Paranoia.

6. It becomes their master status.
7. Typifications.
8. Primary deviance is the initial deviant act itself. Secondary deviance is a result of the label applied to an individual.
9. Canteen culture.
10. They have the ability to decide how they respond to the label.

Crime and Deviance: Marxist Theories of Crime
QUICK TEST (Page 42)
1. Bourgeoisie (ruling class) and proletariat (working class).
2. A full social theory of deviance.
3. Labelling theory.
4. False class consciousness.
5. It suggests that a person's social class is the singular cause of crime.
6. Dr Harold Shipman.
7. Differential association.
8. Laws that restrict a business's ability to make profits.
9. Relative deprivation.
10. It breeds crime in all social classes.

DAY 3

Crime and Deviance: Realism and Crime
QUICK TEST (Page 46)
1. Charles Murray.
2. Broken windows theory.
3. Democratic policing.
4. Conservative political perspective.
5. Biological differences in individuals, such as aggressive personality traits.
6. When a person weighs up the costs of a crime against the rewards of the crime in deciding whether or not to commit it.
7. Relative deprivation.
8. Non-utilitarian crimes such as vandalism.
9. Target hardening.
10. Left realism.

Crime and Deviance: Crime and Gender
QUICK TEST (Page 50)
1. James Messerschmidt.
2. At home, at work and in public.
3. 5 per cent.
4. Expressive role.
5. Hegemonic masculinity.
6. Shoplifting.
7. To work for a living, obtaining a satisfying lifestyle.
8. A lack of a male role model.
9. Chivalry thesis.
10. A bedroom culture.

Crime and Deviance: Crime and Ethnicity
QUICK TEST (Page 54)
1. Macpherson report.
2. Left realists.
3. Philippe Bourgois.
4. Mugging.
5. It is a myth.
6. Over 54,000.
7. Three times more likely.

8. A crisis of capitalism.
9. It doesn't necessarily show that police behaviour on the job will reflect their views shown backstage.
10. Paul Gilroy.

Crime and Deviance: Crime and the Media
QUICK TEST (Page 58)
1. Stanley Cohen.
2. A deviance amplification spiral.
3. News values.
4. Mods and rockers.
5. They were more likely to fear leaving the house at night and falling victim to crime.
6. News displays a false view of which groups are likely to become victims.
7. They believe them to be outdated and too frequent.
8. Due to the vast nature of the internet.
9. Manufactured.
10. 30 per cent.

Crime and Deviance: Globalisation, Crimes of the State and Green Criminology
QUICK TEST (Page 62)
1. One trillion pounds per annum.
2. Harm.
3. Crimes that destroy or degrade the Earth's resources.
4. Deregulation of businesses.
5. Anthropocentric.
6. Risks in society are now global rather than localised and tied to one specific area.
7. Rwanda.
8. Organisations that are locally rooted with global links.
9. McMafia.
10. Businesses have the ability to move production to low-wage countries with less regulations.

DAY 4
Crime and Deviance: Control in Society and Victimisation
QUICK TEST (Page 66)
1. Incapacitation.
2. Panopticon.
3. Victim proneness.
4. Disciplinary power.
5. Popular punitiveness.
6. Broken windows theory.
7. Social and community crime prevention.
8. Restorative justice.
9. Transcarceration.
10. Making a crime harder to perform in order to impact on an individual's rational choice.

Sociological Theory: Quantitative and Qualitative Methodology
QUICK TEST (Page 70)
1. Quantitative data.
2. As it fails to gather informed consent from participants before the research is conducted.
3. The social patterns that exist in society (social facts).

4. It is easily replicated to gather the same results.
5. Governments or other official bodies.
6. Statistics that can be questioned, such as police records.
7. Closed-ended responses.
8. Control group and experimental group.
9. They are conducted in an artificial environment and may cause the Hawthorne effect.
10. They usually follow a standardised procedure.

Sociological Theory: Marxism
QUICK TEST (Page 74)
1. The view that studying society scientifically can provide findings that can be used to better society.
2. Ancient society.
3. The ruling-class ownership and control of ideas and values.
4. Class consciousness.
5. A proletarian revolution.
6. Something that controls thoughts and ideas in order to manipulate the working class into accepting capitalism as a legitimate system.
7. Bourgeoisie.
8. Competition.
9. Dual consciousness.
10. Economic level, political level and ideological level.

Sociological Theory: Functionalism
QUICK TEST (Page 78)
1. Value consensus.
2. Adaptation, goal attainment, integration and latency.
3. Functional alternatives.
4. The organic analogy.
5. Manifest and latent functions.
6. Egoism.
7. Social confusion or normlessness.
8. Institutions.
9. As it is difficult to falsify.
10. Roles in society have their own set of expected norms.

Sociological Theory: Feminism
QUICK TEST (Page 82)
1. Male-led society.
2. Each relationship involves power.
3. Other feminist theories suggest that all women have the same experience of patriarchy.
4. Dual systems feminists.
5. Ways of seeing society.
6. Sex refers to the physical differences between males and females, gender is socially constructed.
7. Marxist feminists.
8. Sylvia Walby.
9. Unconscious ideas of femininity.
10. Equal rights.

DAY 5
Sociological Theory: Social Action Theories
QUICK TEST (Page 86)
1. Micro-level.
2. Animals react instinctively, humans use rational choice.
3. Phenomenology.

4. Indexicality.
5. Rational value-oriented action.
6. Giddens.
7. Impression management.
8. From how we see the impact of our actions on those around us.
9. The situations have consequences.
10. Dramaturgical model.

Sociological Theory: Sociology as a Science
QUICK TEST (Page 90)
1. Gathering evidence to support the claims of a hypothesis.
2. Postmodernism.
3. A paradigm.
4. Free will and consciousness.
5. Verstehen.
6. Quantitative research methods.
7. When there are anomalies.
8. An open system.
9. When a theory or hypothesis is tested repeatedly to see if it can be disproved.
10. Reality.

Sociological Theory: Objectivity and Value Freedom
QUICK TEST (Page 94)
1. To remain free of values.
2. A big story.
3. Max Weber.
4. That they should actively be embraced.
5. That of the underdog.
6. Sociological theory and research that aims to change society for the better.
7. As they will fear that a display of extreme values may hamper future funding.
8. As they became too detached from their research, simply serving their funding bodies.
9. Marxists take a left-wing approach and functionalists take a conservative view of society.
10. Quantitative research methods.

Sociological Theory: Social Policy
QUICK TEST (Page 98)
1. Social problems cause issues for society; sociological problems are simply patterns that call for a sociological explanation, not necessarily negative.
2. Postmodernism.
3. Tax breaks for spouses.
4. The underclass.
5. Relative deprivation.
6. Patriarchy in society.
7. The introduction of refuges for victims of domestic violence.
8. They believe that gradual change as a result of policies is not possible, revolution is needed.
9. Bauman.
10. Zero-tolerance policies.

Sociological Theory: Globalisation, Late-Modern and Postmodern Society
QUICK TEST (Page 102)
1. Modern society.
2. A new way of making profits.

3. What they consume.
4. Signs created by the media have more meaning than reality itself.
5. Meta-narratives.
6. Technological advancements.
7. Countries that control and operate within their own national borders.
8. They see changes made by oppositional groups as reducing inequality in society, rather than a proletariat revolution.
9. Transformative capacity.
10. Individualistic.

DAY 6

Media: The Impact of the New Media
QUICK TEST (Page 106)
1. Those that view the impact of the new media positively.
2. Encouraging greed; dumbed-down content.
3. Habermas.
4. Citizen journalism.
5. Paul Anderson.
6. Digital divide.
7. Herbert Marcuse.
8. They will become less important and eventually disappear.
9. Hyper-real.
10. Baudrillard.

Media: Ownership and Control
QUICK TEST (Page 110)
1. Instrumental or manipulative or traditional Marxism.
2. Bagdikian.
3. Two from religion, family, media or education.
4. Hegemony.
5. Blondel.
6. The idea that active audience choices shape the media.
7. Owners do not interfere; they trust the professionalism of their employees (controllers).
8. There was bias in favour of the bosses and owners.
9. Postmodern.
10. Justifies inequalities caused by capitalism.

Media: Culture and the Media
QUICK TEST (Page 114)
1. Elites or bourgeoisie or higher classes.
2. The experiences of ordinary people.
3. A harsh existence with no time for cultural pursuits.
4. It has become a commodity, anyone can buy it, it is available to all.
5. Academics investigating the rise of totalitarian regimes in Europe.
6. The mass media.
7. Elite culture.
8. Leavis.
9. Postman.
10. Dominant, negotiated, oppositional.

Media: Globalisation, the Media and Culture
QUICK TEST (Page 118)
1. Globalisation.
2. Cultural imperialism.
3. Synergy.
4. Cultural flows theory.
5. Santos.

6. The audience are heterogeneous and active in interpreting media messages.
7. Media messages can be interpreted in many ways.
8. They watch TV now instead of being involved in the community.
9. We live in a media saturated world, exposed to all cultures.
10. We are made sensitive to a plurality of ideas (narratives) because of our exposure to many cultures.

Media: Practical Factors Affecting the Social Construction of the News
QUICK TEST (Page 122)
1. Journalists, editors.
2. Pluralists.
3. Reuters or the Press Association.
4. £466 billion.
5. Leadbetter.
6. Spin.
7. Planning which events will be covered by journalists.
8. Franklin.
9. By calculating how many of the news values a story meets.
10. Marxist.

DAY 7

Media: Ideological Factors Affecting the Social Construction of the News
QUICK TEST (Page 126)
1. Too little time, too few resources.
2. Churnalism.
3. Davies.
4. Corporate values/power elite.
5. Monbiot.
6. Pollution, genocide, sponsorship of military coups.
7. Binary oppositions.
8. The social background of the media professionals (White, middle-class males).
9. Primary definers.
10. The *News of the World* phone-hacking scandal.

Media: Media Representations of Gender and Ethnicity
QUICK TEST (Page 130)
1. By absence, condemnation and trivialisation of women in the media.
2. Laura Mulvey.
3. Abercrombie.
4. Marxism.
5. Active audience models or reception theory.
6. Magazines promoting traditional ideals of womanhood – caring, marriage, family, and how to serve these ideals by looking after others and your own appearance.
7. Using Black actors as an example, aliens in TV shows are portrayed by Black actors; this reinforces ideas of otherness or the perceived essential differences between different groups of people, in this case based on ethnicity (of course no such difference does actually exist).

8. Victims of crime get more media attention if they are White than if they are Black or foreign.
9. Natives, entertainers and slaves (or the newer stereotypes: gangstas, criminals, drug addicts, sports stars, rap or hip hop artists).
10. Dr Haideh Moghissi.

Media: Media Representations of Age and Social Class
QUICK TEST (Page 134)
1. Clockwork Orange Britain.
2. Afro-Caribbean youth.
3. Christopher Lasch.
4. To sell consumer products to help fight against it.
5. Cuddy and Fiske.
6. Marxism.
7. Glasgow University Media Group.
8. Working class or lower social orders or proletariat.
9. *I, Daniel Blake.*
10. Don Heider.

Media: Media Representations of Sexuality and Disability
QUICK TEST (Page 138)
1. Lisa Bennett.
2. Camp.
3. Gross.
4. Pink pound.
5. Normality/abnormality.
6. Competition and proliferation of channels has led to fierce competition, which means the search for bigger audiences and the abandonment of minority programming.
7. Objects of curiosity.
8. 384.
9. Entertain and relieve them of guilt.
10. Glasgow University Media Group (Greg Philo).

Media: Media Effects
QUICK TEST (Page 142)
1. Weak.
2. Copycat violence.
3. Cathartic.
4. Katz and Lazarsfeld.
5. Dominant, negotiated and oppositional.
6. Wallpaper (background), identity (personal issues), our interest in personal relationships and entertainment.
7. 3,500.
8. Bandura, Ross and Ross study into the effects of violent media (Bobo doll experiment).
9. When a person or group of people change behaviour because they know they are being observed (as part of a laboratory experiment).
10. The social group or problem is made worse because of the attention given by the media, more arrests or just an awareness of the activity labelled abnormal.

Index

The author and publisher are grateful to the copyright holders for permission to use quoted materials and images.

Cover and P1: © Cyrick / Shutterstock

P16: Atomazul / Shutterstock; p.28: Albert H. Teich / Shutterstock;
p.96: sciencephoto / Shutterstock

Every effort has been made to trace copyright holders and obtain their permission for the use of copyright material. The author and publisher will gladly receive information enabling them to rectify any error or omission in subsequent editions. All facts are correct at time of going to press.

Published by Letts Educational
An imprint of HarperCollinsPublishers
1 London Bridge Street
London SE1 9GF

ISBN: 9780008179694

First published in 2017

10 9 8 7 6 5 4 3 2 1

British Library Cataloguing in Publication Data.
A CIP record of this book is available from the British Library.

Series Concept and Development: Emily Linnett and Katherine Wilkinson
Commissioning and Series Editor: Katherine Wilkinson
Authors: Andy Bennett, Scott Keifer and Matthew Wilkin
Project Manager: Rachel Allegro
Index: Lisa Footitt
Peer reviewer: Allan Kidd
Cover Design: Paul Oates
Inside Concept Design: Ian Wrigley and Paul Oates
Text design, layout and artwork: QBS Learning
Production: Natalia Rebow
Printed in Italy by Grafica Veneta SpA

MIX
Paper from
responsible sources
FSC
www.fsc.org
FSC™ C007454